INTRODUC

Very few people can work a room like my friend, Joe Pagliei. Whether in a crowd, or talking one-on-one, Joe has always had a way of reeling people in. You could mention a friend's name, a hometown, a place of employment or just about anything, and Joe would find a way to connect. As someone who has made a career out of talking, I could always appreciate Joe's communication skills.

He also threw a heck of party back in his casino days. After attending Joe's golf outings and banquets in Atlantic City, I was well prepared to start hosting my own events. Joe always did everything with style, and I learned well from seeing how he treated everyone with class.

I've now been involved in the organization and presentation of a great number of charity golf outings and other fundraising events in the Philadelphia area for more than 35 years. I have been at it for so long that when I first started, Joe Pagliei was one of the youngest celebrity invitees. In 2017, he's still showing up for most of my events, and now he is just about the oldest participant. Joe is one of those ageless types and the numbers on the birth certificate don't mean a thing. He still fits in with any crowd.

He's never been the biggest name to show up at one of my events, but no one has ever complained about finishing a round of golf or being seated with Joe Pagliei. He's one of those special people who takes an interest in everyone's life, listens to what you have to say and keeps everyone entertained with vintage stories about football, horseracing, the casinos, and of celebrities of all sorts.

He was also a pretty good hustler, but at the same time inscrutably honest. When I was still playing for the Philadelphia Eagles, Joe's wife Rita organized an appearance at Boscov's Department Store. She asked Joe to recruit a couple of Eagles for the event. Joe called Wilbert Montgomery and myself, and said that he had a budget of $2,500 to spend on appearance fees. He told us that he was little tight on cash at the time, so he was going to take a cut and split the money three ways. Wilbert and I figured, what the heck; Joe's a good guy and we were happy to get $800 apiece for showing up. He could have just told us that he had $1,600 to spend and we would have been none the wiser, but he made a point to let us know he was getting a cut.

Joe Pagliei is on the favorite people list of just about everyone who meets him. His mind remains active; he possesses one of the genuinely good souls; and yes, does he have a story for any occasion.

You will enjoy reading about Joe's exploits as much as I've enjoyed hearing Joe talk about them for the past 40 or so years.

Ron Jaworski
September, 2017

TABLE OF CONTENTS

L to R: LeRoy Neiman, Joe Pagliei and Lynn Quale

On the Cover: Joe Pagliei, Tommy Lasorda,
Joe DiMaggio and Joe Torre
Cover art; original portrait of Joe Pagliei
painted by LeRoy Neiman

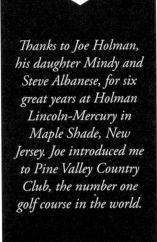

Thanks to Joe Holman, his daughter Mindy and Steve Albanese, for six great years at Holman Lincoln-Mercury in Maple Shade, New Jersey. Joe introduced me to Pine Valley Country Club, the number one golf course in the world.

I – CLAIRTON

The SS Duca d'Aosta was an Italian ocean liner that served the Navazione Generale Italiana from 1908-1929, much of that time sailing a Genoa-Naples-New York route. At capacity it carried about 1,800 passengers. Among those who disembarked at Ellis Island on February 10, 1920, was my father, Alberto Pagliei, formerly of Giuliano, Italy.

There wasn't much to distinguish my father from the other immigrants, except maybe that he was only 14-years old and had made the trip across the ocean by himself. His parents had put him on the boat in Naples headed for Camden, New Jersey where another relative would supposedly have an unspecified job waiting for him.

Alberto stepped off the boat in New York and was pointed in the direction of Camden. He found his way to New Jersey and the prospective employer, but was informed that there were no jobs available, at least not for a 14-year old. He was advised that a number of recent arrivals from Italy were finding work at the US Steel plant in Clairton, located along the Monongahela River in Western Pennsylvania. He boarded a bus with strict instructions from his US handler, that when asked his age, make sure to answer 'diciotto' (18).

He traveled from New Jersey, across Pennsylvania, and got off the bus in the Wilson district of the borough of Clairton. Maybe he did not understand that he had to lie about his age. Maybe he just couldn't lie because he was an honest man his entire life, but when Alberto was again asked his age, he looked his prospective employer in the eye and he replied, "Quattordici." He was told, "Sorry, you're too young, go on home." The problem was that he did not have a home to go to.

My father had his first test of conscience that night.

Alone, broke, jobless and struggling with the language, he realized that maybe a fib was called for. One day older and infinitely wiser, he went back to the US Steel plant and filled out a new application listing 18 as his age. He was told to report to the blast furnace for the first day of what was to become a 48-year career in the janitorial department of US Steel.

Clairton was a thriving company town created by and for the steel industry. While no filming actually occurred there, Clairton was the setting for the 1978 classic film, *The Deer Hunter*. A shot in the opening scene displays a 'Welcome to Clairton, City of Prayer' sign, though the scene was filmed in Mingo Junction, Ohio. While the movie takes place during the Viet Nam Era, the shot-and-a-beer sensibilities of the protagonists reflect a working class-lifestyle that has always defined the people of Clairton.

Around the turn of the century, Carnegie Steel opened a plant in Clairton and soon became the single biggest entity that was absorbed into the newly created US Steel Corporation. This new plant would develop into one of world's largest steel production facilities. Today it remains the largest coke-producing plant in the United

States due to the surrounding Western Pennsylvania coalfields that provide an abundance of bituminous coal that is processed into coke fuel.

Clairton was incorporated as a borough in 1903 and then as a City of Third Class in 1922 and population grew from 6,000 to 15,000 during that decade. While coke was fueling the furnaces at the steel plant, it was also fueling a creation of new jobs and the spike in population. By 1918, the Clairton Works was recognized as the premier coke plant in the nation through the use of an innovative new technology, the by-product coke oven. The oven allowed for the production of coke in a more efficient manner while allowing for the processing of coke-oven gas.

Operating around the clock, the steel mills coated the air with by-product called soot. The air was particularly heavy over my dad's Wilson-Blair neighborhood. That soot seemed to have a presence in nearly all of my childhood memories. It was an ever present mist: a continuous shower that left its mark on houses, cars, bicycles and anything else that was left outside.

Rita DiPasquale married Joe in January 1961. The ever-present soot remains the most lasting memory of her first visit to Clairton:

"My first impression was [to wonder] why the trim on all of the houses was a dark green color. A real grimy dust was present in the air and it settled on all of the houses. Joe explained to me that you had to clean the houses nearly every day."

Like all the other immigrants, my father polished his English at work and hanging around town and he made friends. One family he took a particular interest in was the Ianni's who lived above the grocery store that they operated on State Street, just two doors down from the main entrance gate to the US Steel plant. While the sale of milk, bread and everyday groceries constituted the front-of-the-house operations, it was the activities that occurred in the backroom that distinguished the Ianni family store as a popular neighborhood destination. Behind the grocery shelves during these Prohibition Era years, the proprietors Dominic and Rose would serve up a glass of beer or a shot at a fair and reasonable price. That kindly devoted couple, who would later become my grandparents, operated a speakeasy in the rear quarters of their home and grocery store.

Franklin Roosevelt signed off on the Twenty-first Amendment in 1933, putting an end to Prohibition and making it legal for adults to again consume alcohol. Ianni's had become a popular neighborhood amenity, especially among the steelworkers, and now they could continue to serve their libations without violating any laws.

Nana and Nono's grocery store occupied prime real estate, just feet away from the US Steel entrance that thousands of workers used every day. The millworkers would walk past the store, cross over a railroad bridge, arrive at the gate, show their license and head into work. My grandmother always had shot glasses and whiskey bottles lined up for action at the end of every shift. Drinks were readily available, and as Nana would say, "At the right price." I can recall the steelworkers marching in and out with their lunch buckets tucked under their arms.

As I look back, and having been in so many Wawa's in my time, I now realize that Ianni's may have been the forerunner of the modern convenience store. You could pick up anything that was needed get the family through that night's dinner and maybe breakfast the next day. Need some poultry or a few eggs? Nana and Nono maintained chicken coops out behind the store. Following a long shift at the mill, a steelworker could duck into Ianni's, walk back through the store, visit the chicken coops and hand-pick that night's dinner. While the chicken of choice was being plucked and prepared, the worker could wait at the bar with a cold beer in hand. The chicken would be delivered fresh in a neatly wrapped package of brown paper. The guy might even grab a few eggs and a loaf of bread heading back out through the grocery store.

Alberto Pagliei was among those who commuted back and forth along State Street every day. For him, Ianni's became a regular stop, but it wasn't the groceries, chicken or even beer that kept him coming back. With Rose and Dominic spending so much of their time in the back room and out at the chicken coops, the front grocery section was usually manned by their daughter Elizabeth. As was the case with many girls of that era, the Ianni's had determined that a sixth-grade diploma was a sufficient enough education requirement for Elizabeth and that she would be more useful and productive to the family working in the store.

Attracted to Elizabeth, my father volunteered to help out around the store. There among the groceries, they fell in love. One day Alberto and Elizabeth walked over to City Hall, he took $3 out of his wallet and they left with a marriage license. The first of the their three children, Emily, was born in 1930, followed by sons Joseph in 1934 and Alberto Jr. in 1944. For me, the first son, the family adapted a combined Italian and American pronunciation of my name, and I would be known around Clairton as "Joe-Seffee."

My dad purchased a small two-story house from my aunt and uncle, Frank and Josephine Sorrentino, that he walked past every day on his way to the plant. Aunt Josephine was my mother's sister and the house was just three doors from Ianni's as you headed toward the plant. Frank and Josephine had seven children and my cousin Victor was the master carpenter of the family. He was known around town as 'Vito,' and when Vito had a job, it meant his five brothers also had work. The Sorrentino brothers had built the house for their parents and my dad purchased it from them for $3,500.

Sitting no more than 10 steps from the street, the house featured a ground level floor and a full, finished basement with all the modern conveniences, including a new gas stove and a large 16'x16' kitchen. This kitchen could easily handle 15 or more people and was the main gathering place for large family events. The gas oven also provided heat for the kitchen. Later, when I had my first job in pro football with the Calgary Stampeders, I took some of my pay and surprised my family with two new gas heaters to warm the kitchen. No longer would there be a need for heavy coats and blankets across the lap while dining. We also had a living room and three bedrooms, those spaces all heated by a large potbelly stove. It was my job was to find coal and keep the stove fueled. There were so many coal mines in walking distance of the house, I never had to travel far. I'd walk out the door with a large bucket and within a few minutes I'd be back home with all the free coal we needed. I'd empty a bucket into the street level coal chute and head back out for another load.

My father was a practical man, so he moved our family into the three-bedroom basement and rented the top floor to a local businessman named Moe Martin. Moe paid $35 a month in rent and operated a business designed to provide a recreational outlet for the hardworking steelworkers. Moe recognized that our real estate provided a convenient location for those steelworkers who wished to play the daily number, shoot a round of pool or sit in on a poker game before or after work. Moe's take was a 5% vig on all of the funds that exchanged hands in his venue. He stashed his cash in a wall safe that was concealed by nothing more than a calendar. It was years later when a friend told me the story about the safe behind the calendar and I learned that I was probably the only person in town who didn't know about it; apparently it was common knowledge. The mill shifts started and ended around the clock and, from what I remember, Moe seemed to be always open for business. I don't know when he slept, but he didn't miss a single opportunity to collect a buck.

Because my bedroom was located in the basement below the poker room, I never needed bedtime stories to fall asleep. Most nights I dozed off listening to tales of woe that worked their way down from Moe's. After a while, the voices became recognizable and I always knew who was being dealt all the wrong cards on that particular night.

> *Jim Kelly, a native of Clairton and neighbor of the Pagliei family, would go on to become an All-American end at Notre Dame where he caught passes from both John Huarte and Daryle Lamonica. He was drafted by both the Pittsburgh Steelers (NFL) and Boston Patriots (AFL) in the second round of the 1964 draft. He played professionally for both the Steelers and the Philadelphia Eagles:*
> *"We lived on a hill above Joe's house, 106 steps from my door to his. He lived below a pool hall and I used to watch guys going in and out of there all day and night. Joe slept about 25 yards away from the train tracks. Our town was known as the Coke Capital of the world and you would have trains constantly about, carrying about 200 loads a day. He lived right off the tracks and the trains would shake his bedroom as they went by."*

The most distinctive feature in our backyard was a round metal barrel that was propped up on cinder blocks and always had a fire burning in it, day after day, all year round. This barrel was essential to Moe's operation as it served as the repository for all of the daily number receipts and other potentially incriminating documents. These ashes would become one and the same with the soot that drifted down from the mill smokestacks.

The back border of our yard was delineated by what was simply known as 'the tracks,' about six sets of rail lines that ran south into Pittsburgh and north to points beyond Elizabeth that took them off of my personal geographic chart. Elizabeth was the end of my world and any place existing past there exceeded my boundaries of knowledge. Behind the tracks stood the seemingly never-ending mass that made up the US Steel Plant. The plant operated three shifts around the clock, seven days a week and to meet that demand, the tracks were always hopping with activity.

While the house that served as home to the Pagliei family it seemed to be plenty big enough for Joe when he was growing up, it didn't seem quite so large to his daughter Patti when she visited years later as a young girl, but the people and the color of the town lived up to her father's stories:

"As a child I only visited the house where my dad grew up in once, and I couldn't believe how tiny it was. I loved it! Making homemade gnocchi with my granny and siblings while mom and dad visited the local friends. It was such a wonderful, colorful world… full of scents and stories and memories. It somehow felt more authentic than our home in NJ. I loved listening to my grandparents speaking broken Italian, and more so, loved eating the delicious Italian meals prepared by hand and from their own garden.

"I always loved when Dad would tell stories about his old friends from the neighborhood… the Italians, with names like 'Skinny Phil' and 'Tony with The Sausages' (not to be confused with the other Tonys in the 'hood). These first-born Italian-Americans were like characters out of "Goodfellas" or "The Sopranos." Stories about their exploits, their cars, the time they met Sinatra… and when they were up on their luck or down on their luck. Tales of the sons and daughters of immigrants that felt more like scenes from a movie rather than real life. It was a really special moment in time."

While growing up, I especially enjoyed the perks that came with having my grandparents operate a grocery store. With the store just two doors from my house, I was there every day. I look back with some regret when I realized I could have been in on the ground floor of the baseball card boom. The Topps company introduced its first version of the baseball card in 1949. Single cards were included as premiums in packages of gum. There were current players such as Hank Greenberg, Ralph Kiner and Bob Feller, along with special cards featuring the likes of Babe Ruth, Ty Cobb and Honus Wagner. I was allowed to take one pack of that gum a day. If I took more, my grandmother Rose would chase me out of the store. I wish I had those cards today, no doubt they'd be worth nice sum of money. I like to think that it was other members of my family who lost or misplaced them so that I feel less remorseful.

On his days off from the steel mill my father would take me over to West Virginia to visit Charleston Racetrack. This is where I first developed what would become a lifelong fondness for the ponies. I developed a natural feel for horses and horse people, and these traits would serve me well when I became a jockey agent later on. I was probably exposed to less gambling at the track than I was in everyday life in Clairton. I had Moe Martin operating his business beneath the same roof I lived under and, if I stepped outside, within a few blocks I could find just about any game of chance.

Clairton was a big-time gambling town when I was growing up. We weren't allowed to have anything to do with Moe's or any of the other places, but gambling was all around. I used to sit on the top step and watch all of the action in Moe's. Every imaginable betting game: Craps; Blackjack; Draw Poker; Barboot, which was a form of craps; Greek style, played on a pool table with dice; pool; you name it. If it involved cards or dice, you could find it.

There was group of about six guys, all friends, who worked as a team to 'get the money.' These guys had the best cheating schemes in the world. Nobody could come into town and win consistently. They had it all figured and could change the odds so the dice fell in their favor, marked cards and loaded dice that could produce a '7' or 'crap out' when needed.

The main guys were Puppy, Benedetto, Josie Ankoral and the Flattop Giangarlo. They controlled and ran the dice and card games in town and there were pool sharks at all the tables. Eight ball, nine ball, it didn't matter, all the guys at the steel mill were making a good living. Many of them would stop in on payday and some of them would lose their whole paychecks. Puppy's place was known as 'the joint,' and when some of the married guys lost all their money the wives would come in and complain to Puppy. He would return the money and tell the wives to let their husbands know that they were never allowed back in 'the joint' again.

It seemed in Clairton that if you weren't working at US Steel, you were writing numbers, making sports book, or doing some form of hustling. Whether you lived in town or were just visiting, you could find any kind of action. But to be sure, the odds were never in your favor. Clairton was a crude, rust belt version of Las Vegas. I saw so much losing around me that one of the takeaways from my childhood was that gambling was a sickness and that money is better off in your pocket than on a table. Later, when I was working at the busiest casinos in Atlantic City, I was able to view gambling through clear, dispassionate eyes and I never got caught up in the action. For me it was just another business.

Except for the occasional trip to the racetrack, my father kept his money in his pocket. Every morning he would get up, pick out one of his four sets of union suit underwear, fasten the trap door and head to the mill. Indoor showers were just beginning to find their way into the homes of Clairton and, until I was 13, we all took turns taking baths in a big wash tub.

The first shower I ever took was at Walnut Junior High School. I stepped into the shower and stared at the fixtures, I didn't know how to work it. Somebody showed me how to turn it on and I went home and told my father about it. He was so impressed that he called Toto Magaro, the local plumber, and had him come over and install one in our basement apartment. What a pleasure to take a warm shower in my own home!

Showers were not my only first at Walnut JHS. It was there that I learned that real footballs were not made out of towels and tape. I had been playing football on the streets and at the playground for as I long as I could remember, but we 'made' our footballs. I was always big and fast for my age and generally got into games with older kids. Football and baseball were always popular. We discovered basketball one day in my backyard when we took the top hoop from one of Moe Martin's old sheet-burning barrels and nailed it to a square of wood, a carefully measured 10' off the ground. Once we got good enough on my home court we moved on to the Third Street playground. I loved basketball, but was never known for my shooting touch. I was a rebounder and I guess the best way to describe my game is that I knocked the shit out of everybody.

We also fitted my backyard out with a horseshoe pit and we took care of it like greenskeepers at a country club. The 2'x2' boxes were measured to the hair and filled with regulation clay. The pit was watered daily and covered with canvas when it wasn't in use. Of course, the horseshoes conformed to all official specs. I developed lifelong friendships around that horseshoe pit with guys John "Tiggy" Tenaglia, Arnold "Spider" Rondenelli and Nello "Tubby" Fiore.

I was seven years old when Pearl Harbor was attacked, December 7, 1941.

It seemed that all of the men in Clairton who were of conscription age stood by their mailboxes waiting to see if this was the day they received their 'Greetings From Uncle Sam' notice. Like in so many other towns across the country, many of the guys took the initiative to get in on the action and went downtown and enlisted. Almost overnight the streets were filled with men in uniform and the smell of Camel cigarettes was in the air. It seemed like it was mandatory for all the recruits to smoke and in the pictures of my mind, they all have Camels hanging off their lips and a cold beer in one hand.

The other men who were of draft age that received a 4-F 'not acceptable for service in the Armed Forces' classification were known around town as '2nd Story Rats.' These guys spent most of the war trying to show care for the wives whose husbands were off serving the country. They seemed to live by the edict of 'get in, get it and get out' when it came to watching over the women. Later, when the war was over, the veterans would get together on Clairton Hill and exchange war stories. The 4-F guys would also get together and talk about their war-time adventures.

One indelible memory was the period from mid-August 1945, when the Japanese formally surrendered, and the official VJ Day commemoration on September 2, which effectively ended World War II. It was like one big ongoing end-of-summer party in Clairton. My whole family was out in the streets with the rest of the town. We celebrated with the troops, the veterans, the bands, the Daughters of the American Revolution: there were parades of marchers, fire trucks, police cars and hot rods. It was like a scene from a movie, I'll never forget that time. The whole town seemed re-energized with the war having finally come to an end. The steel mills were pumping around the clock and there was so much action in the streets.

I continued playing every type of ball all over town and, when it was time enter Clairton High School, those older guys that I had been playing with all along encouraged me to go out for the football team. I weighed about 185 pounds, which was big for a running back in those days. Serb Matich was the backfield coach and he also taught me to punt. Every night we would go down to the coal pile and punt the ball to each other. I would be a punter on every team that I played on through high school, college, military and pro ball.

We had a lot of great athletes in our neighborhood. Jim Kelly, who had a great career as a tight end at Notre Dame in the early 1960's and later played professionally for the Steelers and Eagles, grew up right across the street from me. He lives in South Jersey now and I still run into him at various functions. He always tells people that I was his hero when he was growing up.

I played sports year round at Clairton High and my junior and senior years I started on the football, basketball and baseball teams. Football was my first love, but it was baseball that offered me my first shot at turning pro. The Boston Braves scouted me and were impressed enough to try and sign me to a contract to play for their minor league team in Indianapolis. I appreciated the opportunity, but it really wasn't tough to turn the Braves down as football was always my first love. I would continue to play baseball through my freshman year at Clemson. I started in centerfield, batted .367 and the team made it to Omaha for the College World Series. One of my great thrills was playing an American Legion game at Forbes Field, home of the Pittsburgh Pirates, and hitting a home run off of the iron gate in left field. Yes, I have often wondered if I could have made it all the way to the Braves if I had accepted that contract but, as a teenager, all I really cared about was football.

Jim Kelly recalls Joe as a baseball player:
"My father, Harry Kelly, coached the American Legion team for guys Joe's age. I was, seven-, eight-years old, and was the batboy for the team. My father worked nights at the steel mill, everyone worked at the steel mill. Joe could hit the ball. There was a street that ran behind the outfield and the outfielders would have to stop and wait for cars for pass before they could chase after the ball."

My senior year I received recruitment letters from 105 colleges. I had made the All-W.P.I.A.L team, All-Western Pennsylvania, and received other honors and recognition as a senior running back. The recruiting process was nothing like it is today, I didn't visit a single campus. Maybe a coach, a former player from the area or someone else connected to the program might make a phone call or stop by the house for a visit, but that was the extent of the personal contact. I got letters from all over the country but, I have to admit, I didn't know much about most of those schools or even where they were located. At 18-years old I had still never travelled beyond Western Pennsylvania and any knowledge I had of any of the schools was limited to whether or not I was familiar with their football program.

Jim Kelly recalls the effect football had on the town of Clarion:
"The whole town was about football. In those days the population was about 20,000. Now it's about 8,000. You'd get crowds of about six or seven thousand

and the town and county police would bring horses down on the field to keep the crowds back. The stands would be full and people would be six or seven deep around the sidelines. The football was very competitive. It was the Steel Valley League with schools like Monongahela, Mahoning, Aliquipa and Mckeesport. It was the best league in Pennsylvania. Clairton is still about football. The makeup of the team has changed, but they had a streak a few years ago that was about 67 straight games won. The teams is mostly African-American now, but the quality of the kid hasn't changed. We had about five or six African-Americans in the whole school, but football is part of the culture. It doesn't matter who you are, if you are from Clairton, you play football. Football at Clairton holds the town together. Clairton was all about football. The stadium was about fifteen blocks from the high school, and you would look for the players walking by with their letter jackets. It was exciting, everyone in town knew the football players.

"For years there was a bus driver named Flat Top who used to drive the football team to all of the away games. He was mixed up with gambling and he would ask us all the time, 'what'd you think, what'd you think?' Everybody was betting on the games. We'd be getting on the bus and he would be pumping us for information.

"I remember people talking about Joe. He was big and strong and fast and just ran over people. He was the punter and had a real strong leg. I remember the fathers talking about him. He was eight years my senior. He was a hell of an athlete. He still hits the golf ball further than guys who are fifty.

"Even today everyone in Clairton knows Joe Pags. That's what he's known as. He knows more people than anyone I know. He was real close with Bob Pellegrini. I remember one of my high school basketball games, he had been a star at Clemson and everyone was talking that he brought Bob Pellegrini and the two of them were in the stands for our game. They told us that Joe was here to watch us play. After the game he and Pelly came into our locker room. Pelly was one of his best friends. Joe came over and told me I played a good game. It was a big deal to have Joe Pagliei and Bob Pellegrini at our game."

I had taken mostly vocational courses in high school and had not given much thought to college. We didn't have a telephone in the house and my high school coach suggested we get one to handle the college calls. We were having dinner one night and we're all startled when the phone begins to ring. The phone was new and this was an unfamiliar sound in house. Hardly anyone we knew had a phone, so there was no one for us to call or receive call from. We looked at the phone and looked at each other, none of us had ever answered a telephone. My father said he would handle it and gets up, takes the receiver and puts it to his ear. The voice on the other end asks, "Is Joe there?" My father answers, "Yes" and he hangs up the phone. He didn't know that he was supposed continue the conversation and then hand the phone over to me.

The Monongahela Valley, which included Clairton, was always a hotbed for college recruiter, players from our area could be found on campuses all over the country. My final three choices for college came down to Florida State, University of Miami and Clemson, for no other reason than I liked the football coaches at each school and they seemed to want me the most. I chose Clemson and prepared for my first trip to another region of the country.

One of the more local colleges that had recruited me was Penn State. A young assistant coach named Joe Paterno called and paid me a visit. Years later when I was working at Harrah's, I flew out to Canton, Ohio along with one of my high rollers and one of Harrah's executives. I was getting ready for dinner when I got a call from the Harrah's guys telling me to hurry down, that Joe Paterno was in the house and the high roller wanted to meet him. I hustled down and went over to Joe and introduced myself. I stuck out my hand and said "Coach, Joe Paglie…" and before I could get another word out, Paterno said, "Clairton, Pennsylvania; I tried to recruit you." I'm thinking, 'what a memory he has.'

I was pretty ambivalent about going to college. I knew I wanted to play football, but I really didn't want to go to school. I was in love at the time and wasn't sure I wanted to move away. The one college that kept after me persistently was Clemson. I was pretty sure I was going to take a job at the steel mill and let the college recruiting letters pile up, unopened on a table. In Clairton, the most common high school graduation gift was a lunch bucket, something that most of my classmates expected to be carrying to the job every day for the rest of their working lives. My father didn't want to hear any talk about working at the steel mill and finally said to me in Italian, "You no go to-a college; you no-a my son." College wasn't on my radar at the time but, with my father pushing me, I dumped the girlfriend and accepted the Clemson scholarship offer.

Clairton was certainly good to me. I can't say that I regret never living there as an adult but, growing up in a hard-nosed steel town, I was ready for anything. I'm soon to be honored as a Forever Son of Clairton. In September of this year, 2017, I was inducted into the Clairton Hall of Fame.

My brother Al Junior, my father Albert Pagliei, my mother Elizabeth and me

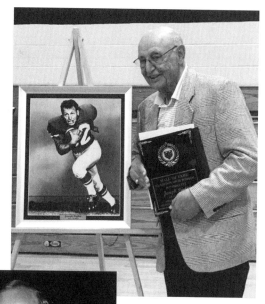

Clairton induction to the Hall of Fame

Joe Pagliei (right) with father Albert & mother Elizabeth

Sam Pacich
"Ding Ding"
Vocational ... steering committee 3 ... has a great interest in automobiles, dances, and girls ... school doesn't agree with him ... hopes to make a lot of money fast.

Fred Fage
Academic ... track 4 ... has a noteworthy collection of stamps ... finds all forms of sciences and mathematics interesting ... would like to study at Carnegie Institute of Technology.

Joseph Pagliei
"Joltin' Joe"
Vocational ... football 2,3, 4; basketball 2,3,4; baseball 3,4; Varsity Club 2,3; Student Council 2,4, vice-president; steering committee 4 ... looks forward to coaching ... favorite pastimes are sports and a certain girl.

John Parach
"Johnny"
Academic ... band 2,3,4; track 2,3 ... gets a kick out of taking things apart and trying to put them back together ... Johnny will learn the plumbing trade.

Daniel Pastore
"Garibaldi"
Commercial ... football 2, 3; baseball 2 ... his favorite pastime is standing in front of the pool room watching the girls go by ... hopes to marry and have lots of kids.

Ronald Pastore

Club; newspaper 4; trying staff ... likes to curl up in a chair on a rainy day with a good book and an apple.

Joe Pagliei V.P. Student Government

Two representatives from each senior home room form the Senior Council to guide the seniors through thick and thin. This group coordinates the Senior Class functions and makes them a success.

Junior Council makes a hit in selecting its class ring design and arranging the Junior-Senior Prom. Composed of two students from each junior home room, they revise the Handbook, a guiding light to prospective sophomores.

Student Council handles problems common to the student body as a whole, and is therefore a representation of each home room in Senior High School.

STUDENT COUNCIL OFFICERS
Sitting: Thomas Nikolich, president.
Standing: Joseph Pagliei, vice-president, Viola Roberts, secretary-treasurer.

2 – CLEMSON

In the summer of 1952, my father put me on a train for Clemson, South Carolina. The only time I had ever left Western Pennsylvania was to cross over the state border into West Virginia. As a high school senior, I had received over 100 recruitment letters and was visited by about 5 recruiters, but had never visited any of the schools.

I had no plans for the future and had exerted even less thought to what I was looking for in a curriculum. I simply wanted to go to a school that would allow me to play both football and baseball. I knew little about what was then known as Clemson Agricultural and Military College. I didn't realize until I got down to South Carolina that the 'M' in Clemson A&M stood for 'Military.' I went there because they seemed to want me the most. Clemson was a 'boys only' school in those days. I wasn't aware that there wouldn't be any coeds on campus and, truthfully, that might have affected my decision if I had known ahead of time. I had absolutely no military aspirations, but I had been admitted to the school as a Reserve Officer Training Corp (ROTC) cadet, one of approximately 3,000 in my freshman class. I was quickly introduced to the fact that the university people took their history and traditions very seriously. First day on campus we were taken to the beautiful house that had served as the home to both John C. Calhoun and the family of his son-in-law, university founder Thomas Clemson. Calhoun had been a statesman who served as vice president to both John Quincy Adams and Andrew Jackson. The Clemson family had purchased Chilium Castle Manor Estate after the death of Calhoun and established Clemson Agricultural College in 1889. As a Yankee from Western Pennsylvania, I wasn't really impressed with all of this 'Mr. Calhoun' reverence or how our campus guides made a big deal of southern tradition. In the 1950's people around Tiger Town still talked proudly of their Rebel heritage, all I cared about was the location of the football and baseball fields.

Because I had been a vocational student at Clairton High, I was short a few academic credits when I got to Clemson and thus had to take summer school classes. As part of my music appreciation class, I had to attend a classical music concert in Atlanta and I didn't know how to dress or behave at such an event. Coach Frank Howard told me to wear a jacket and tie and just watch the crowd. Clap when everyone else clapped, stand up when everyone else stands up, etc. "I followed Coach Howard's instructions and played 'Simon Says' throughout my night at the opera and followed the lead of those seated around me. When it was over I ripped off my tie and never went back to another classical musical event again'.

As a football player, I arrived on campus a week or so ahead of the other freshman in order to begin training camp. I was assigned a room with a sophomore cadet, John Profit. I was expected to perform 'Rat Service' for him, which meant that I was his personal valet: cleaning up after him, making his bed and following his instructions. They even handed me a Clemson beanie which I was supposed to wear everywhere on campus. Second day on campus, I received my uniform and military gear; everything except a pair of shiny patent leather shoes which my father had to send to me.

I have to admit that I really wasn't prepared for the military aspects of the curriculum and had a tough time dealing with the regimented stuff. I put up with it as best I could, but I was only there for the sports.

Frank Howard was a colorful character and one of the more prominent coaches in college football during his tenure as head coach at Clemson from 1940-1969. I was there right in the middle of his career, while he was growing the program from small college obscurity to that of a major national player. When asked why he retired after the 1969 season, Howard would answer, "It was for health reasons: the alumni got sick of me." Today the Tigers play their home games on Frank Howard Field. He had a record of 165-118-2 at Clemson and won six Atlantic Coast Conference championships. He played in six bowl games between 1949 and 1959; unfortunately none of them occurred during my time there. In fact, Coach Howard took the Tigers to bowl games the year before I arrived and the year after I left. I would go on to have a good career, but I certainly wasn't any kind of good luck charm.

Coach Howard was a great coach and helped me get my head screwed on right, he understood how to handle me. I wasn't the first or last of his recruits who had total disdain for the military regimentation, but I doubt that anybody hated the ROTC more than me. As soon as I got on the football field, I felt at home. I started at halfback and did the punting for the freshman team. During my four years at Clemson I was usually the biggest running back on the team and, during my first year, I made a name for myself as a strong, bullish runner.

After two weeks of training camp, classes started. We awoke to reveille at 6 every morning, dressed in our uniforms and marched around the Military Quadrangle. All of this training no doubt came in handy a few years later when I was playing for Team Uncle Sam, but I hated every minute of the soldier business when I was at Clemson. I wasn't very good at it, didn't want to be good at it, and no doubt it showed. About one month into that first semester I called Wally Butts, the head coach at the University of Georgia. Wally had recruited me, and when I got him on the phone I told him that he had to get me out of here and that I would be on my way to Georgia. I got on the train, made my way to Athens and met with Coach Butts in his office. We talked for a few minutes and he picked up the phone and called Coach Howard at Clemson and said to him, "I have that crazy Italian running back of yours sitting in my office, what do you want me to do?" Howard's response was, "Send the crazy bastard back here, I need him." That ended my transfer plans.

I went in to see Coach Howard, not knowing what to expect. I told him how miserable I was and that if I had known about the ROTC responsibilities beforehand I never would have accepted his scholarship offer. He listened, then told me to get out of his office but stick around campus. A short while later I received notice that I was being transferred out of the military dorm and now had a new home in The Field House, where most of the married students lived. That move made all the difference. I stayed and loved every minute of the Clemson experience.

One reason I felt at home at Clemson was that I was always surrounded by teammates from Western Pennsylvania. That area had become a fertile recruiting ground for Clemson. Most of the guys on the roster were from the Deep South but, outside of that, we always had a nucleus of players from the coal region. Ray Mathews, who I became friendly with, was few years older than me and was from McKeesport. He had a great career at Clemson and became a star receiver for the Pittsburgh Steelers throughout the 1950's. Happy with the results they got from Ray, the Clemson coaches kept coming back to Pennsylvania and during my years at Clemson I played with guys like Walt Laraway, Dick Merazza, Leon Kaltenbach, Dick DeSimone, Bill Tosh and Bob Paredes, who all came from Western PA.

We had a good freshman team. The varsity had a down year, going only 2-6-1, but things were expected to improve when our team moved up the following season. The NCAA did not allow freshman to play varsity football until 1968.

For whatever reason, freshmen were allowed to play varsity baseball and that spring I became Clemson's starting centerfielder. We had a good season and I hit about .365. I was having a great time, but near the end of the season Coach Howard came to one of our games and told me that he didn't like the way I had just slid into second base. He pulled me aside and told me that I had to quit the baseball team because I was going to break an ankle sliding like that. He said that he needed me healthy on the football field and added, "A punter can't punt with a bad ankle."

Maybe it's a good thing Coach Howard got me off the baseball field, as I would become the starting right halfback midway through my sophomore year and go on to lead the ACC in punting average all three of my varsity seasons. We finished with a record of 3-5-1 in 1953, but we believed that things were on the upswing and the following season would be more successful since the guys who were part of a good freshman team would now have a full season of varsity experience.

We were marginally better in 1954, going 5-5. I was the starting right halfback and broke some big pass plays out of the backfield that year. I led the team in yardage per reception, with 28.9 yards per catch.

My senior year, 1955, we started out 3-0 and were ranked 16th in the country by the Associated Press going into game four against Rice. We were giving some serious thought to ourselves as potential ACC champs until we got down to Houston and the Owls handled us 21-7; that knocked us out of the rankings for good. We did win our next two games to get to 5-1, but played ranked teams the following two games. We lost to Maryland, which was #2 in the country at the time, 25-12; then #14 Auburn beat us 21-0. Our team finished with a record of 7-3, good for third place in the ACC. I averaged 6.0 yards per carry my senior year, rushing for 476 yards, and had another big year catching passes, averaging 23.3 on 10 receptions. The following year Coach Howard went 7-2-2 and took the Tigers to the Orange Bowl, where they lost to Colorado 27-21.

My picture in the 1955 program carried the following notation:

Joe Pagliei was Clemson's regular right halfback most of last fall and half of 1953. The

Cavaliers hault PAGLIEI after six-yard gain.

CLEMSON 0
AUBURN 21

Auburn, who had never beaten Clemson in Ladd Stadium were looking for a bowl bid and things went sweet for the Plainsmen as they eyed the Cotton Bowl or the Sugar Bowl with a 21 to 0 victory over the Tigers.

Auburn's first score came via a 40-yard pass play in the first quarter. Bob James drove over from the three for their second score and Tubbs ran the belly-play over from the four for the last six points.

O'DELL gained 74 yards to pass the 1,000 mark in his college career, going to a total of 1,073. DICK MARAZZA and WINGO AVERY were the outstanding linesmen in the Clemson forward wall.

Whereas the Plainsmen had completely dominated play in the first half, Clemson picked themselves up and came back to outplay the black jerseyed Plainsmen. The Bengals moved 82 yards in the third quarter as KING directed a drive trying to get back in the ball game. After 17 plays had carried the ball to the Auburn one, an in-motion penalty stopped the Clemson surge. This was the first time the Tigers had failed to score since being blanketed by Maryland in 1954.

Halfback, JOE PAGLIEI, should have remembered the old saying, "He who hesitates is lost."

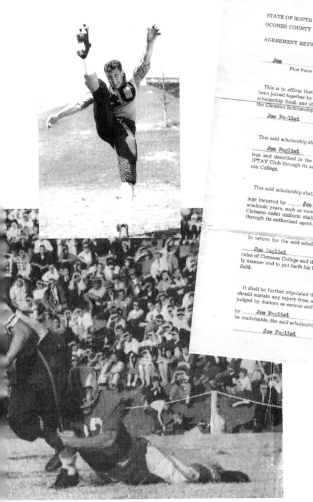

Stars for Clemson

Joe Paglici of Clairton is a varsity outfielder for Clemson although only a freshman. He is the second leading hitter on the team with a .357 mark. Clemson won the South Carolina collegiate title and was runner-up in the Southern Conference. Paglici also stood out at left half for Clemson in spring *biggest back on the team, he led the ACC in punting in 1954. Is a flashy performer.'*

One of the nation's big rivalry games is the Clemson-South Carolina grudge match. In that rivalry I still hold the record for the longest touchdown catch by a Tiger. I hooked up with Joel Wells for an 81 yard catch-and-run in 1952. That play still keeps my name in the archives of the great 'Carolina-Clemson' rivalry.

Coach Frank Howard
and Grandchild.
Famous Rock – "Don't touch
my rock unless you give 100%
on the football field."

3 – CALGARY

I was passed over in the 1956 NFL draft, but did receive free agent invitations from the Green Bay Packers and Washington Redskins, neither offer coming with any form of guarantee. I also got a call from the Calgary Stampeders of the Canadian Football Council. Head coach Jack Hennemier had been the defensive line and 'chief defensive coach' at the University of Maryland from 1948-1954, a stint which included a national championship in 1953. He left Maryland to take over the Stampeders in 1955.

I had a nice career and was hoping to get drafted. The only thing I really wanted to do in life was play football. My coaches at Clemson thought I had a shot, but the whole draft process was still stuck in the pre-historic stages in the mid-1950's. As collegiate players, we weren't heavily scouted, I think most pro personnel guys got their information off of stat sheets by reading The Sporting News.

Hennemier was aggressive in recruiting US imports for his team. Maryland defeated Clemson in each of my three varsity seasons with the Tigers, but I played well in the games and must have left a positive impression. My initial Stampeders recruitment call actually came from Bob Pellegrini, who had been an All-American at Maryland.

Pelly called and told me that a bunch of guys were getting together and going up to Calgary to play for Jack Hennemeier. I told him that sounded good, count me in. When I got there, I was the only one of the American players who showed. Pelly and the other guys all went straight to the NFL. When I did talk to Hennemeir, he assured me I was wanted, said that he needed a good running back and punter from the United States and that I was their man.

They had offered me a better contract than the Packers or Redskins: a package that was about $10,200, which included a 15% bonus and 15% up front. This was a dream come true. I told them by phone that I accepted their offer and when I hung up the first thing I did was look for Calgary on the map. I knew nothing about Calgary, Canada or the league that was known at that time as the Canadian Football Council. This was the forerunner of what was to become the Canadian Football League in 1958.

Hennemier's 1955 Stampeders team had finished last in the Western Division with a record of 4-12. He was pulling out all the stops to avoid a similar record in 1956 and was going after everybody that played US collegiate football. Forrest Gregg had been captain of the 1955 SMU Mustangs team and a second round draft pick of the Green Bay Packers. Hennemier flew to Dallas to persuade him to come up to Canada. Hennemier was dead serious, though I'm not so sure Gregg gave any real consideration to the offer. When he brought the Calgary offer back to the Packers, they told him that they weren't going to match it and that he was free to go. Gregg signed with Green Bay and would go on to become, in the words of Vince Lombardi, "The finest player

I ever coached." In February of '55, Hennemier was sued by the Washington Redskins for attempting to sign two of their players who had also played at Maryland, Dick Modzliewski and Bob Morgan. Jack Hennemier was undoubtedly aggressive, but his efforts went for naught. Poor Jack didn't even make it to October, he was fired on September 19 with a record of 2-5.

So here I am in Canada. The coach who recruited me was fired about two months into the season and the players who gave me the pep talk and all promised to join in never showed up. Looked like the joke was on me, but to this day I have no complaints, that season in Calgary was a great experience although, in the end, we again finished last in the Western Division.

The team trained at a resort in Banff, near the River of No Return where Marilyn Monroe and Robert Mitchum had filmed a movie by that name in 1954. We played two games a week from August to October to get the season in because winter comes early in Canada and the weather gets bad rather quickly. We had potbelly stoves in the locker room to keep warm.

Our quarterback was Don Klosterman, who would go on to become better known as a very successful executive in three leagues, the AFL, NFL and later the USFL. His move from the playing field to the front office was hastened by an accident he suffered on the slopes in Banff while he was still active with the Stampeders. In trying to avoid another skier, he smacked into a tree and damaged his spinal column. There was talk that he might be permanently paralyzed from the accident but, though he would never play football again, he was walking with a cane within a year.

My favorite teammate in Calgary was an end named Sugarfoot Anderson. When we were training in Banff, he sneaked a girl into camp in the trunk of his car and smuggled her into his room. This was the stuff that legends are made of.

I had to get used to the differences in the field: 110 yards; 20 yard end zones and; 55 yards wide, but I was productive for my one season in Canada, averaging 5.7 yards for 324 yards on 57 carries, with three touchdowns. I was also the team's primary punter, averaging 37.7 yards on 64 kicks. We were only allowed 12 US players on the team and, with Hennemier fired, management got rid of all of us at the end of the season.

Looking back I sometimes regret not pursuing one of the NFL offers and trying to get into the league earlier, but I just wanted to play football and Calgary offered me more money than I ever thought I could make playing ball.

The Stampeders cut me and from there I would have no say in trying to make another roster. Uncle Sam took care of that decision for me. I received notice that off-season my professional football career was being put on hold and the next team I would be playing for would be the US Army: home field, Fort Knox, Kentucky.

4 – EAGLES

The Philadelphia Eagles opened training camp for the 1959 season in Hershey, Pennsylvania in July. The team had been only 2-9-1 the year before and had, in fact, been pretty dismal for most of the 1950's. The Eagles won their second consecutive NFL championship in 1949, but mostly lean and downright disappointing seasons followed. I was new to the program but I can tell you, the guys that I was joining up with did not in any way resemble a pack of losers. Everybody was upbeat and optimistic and I was soon to find out that this was a most special bunch of football players who, in a short time, would come to define what it really meant to be a team.

I didn't know much about the Eagles organization when I joined the team as I had never really watched much professional football. I was always playing, whether it was Clairton, Clemson, Calgary or Fort Knox, and didn't follow any other teams than my own. When I got to Philadelphia, I learned that things had started to change for the better prior to the '58 season. The team had undergone about as big a facelift as a franchise can undergo in a single offseason. When the 1958 season opened, just about everything that mattered was new: new home stadium, new coach, and most important, a new and special quarterback. In my opinion it was the quarterback that really made the difference in turning around the fortunes of the franchise.

In very short order, following the last game of 1957, The Eagles vacated Connie Mack Stadium and moved into Franklin Field on the campus of the University of Pennsylvania as their new home stadium. They also fired head coach Hugh DeVore. After flirting with, and being rejected by, a New York Giants assistant named Vince Lombardi, they were able to lure Buck Shaw, a veteran NFL coach, out of retirement. These moves were significant, but the real franchise changer was a trade with the Los Angeles Rams that brought future Hall of Fame quarterback Norm "Dutch" Van Brocklin to Philadelphia. The acquisition of Van Brocklin bumped another future Hall of Famer, Sonny Jurgensen, to the bench.

Van Brocklin made the Eagles an exciting team on offense. During the '58 season, the Eagles developed one of the best passing games in the league with Dutch throwing to a receiving crew that had Tommy McDonald and Pete Retzlaff on the outside, and Bobby Walston at tight end. They were also deep at running back, so it was a pretty successful offense that I was looking to join in 1959.

The Eagles had scouted me at Fort Knox, liked what they saw and offered me a contract for the 1958 season and I accepted. I wasn't able to secure my discharge, but I finished up my military obligation knowing that I was officially part of the Eagles organization. To this day, I'm still fighting with the NFL trying to get pension credit for the season that I was under contract but had to finish up my military commitment. One of my Army teammates was linebacker Bob Pellegrini, who had been an All-American at the University of Maryland and was drafted in the fourth round by the Eagles in 1956. Twelve players from that Army team would go on to play in the NFL, to give you an idea of the talent we put on the field, and we were always being followed by scouts and other league personnel. The Eagles sent several scouts and coaches down to keep an eye on their draft pick, Pellegrini, and it was Pelly who recommended me to the team. I had played against Pelly and Maryland in college. They always beat us, but I usually played well in those games. The Eagles helped me get my discharge from the Army and I was on my way to join the team for training camp.

I was discharged from the Army in May of '59 and headed back to Clairton to prepare for a real NFL training camp. I knew that I had to get myself into better shape but didn't have a specific program to follow. Off-season personal training was unheard of in the 1950's. Most of the guys couldn't afford to take time to work out and money was so meager in those days that just about every player worked other jobs between football seasons. When I got to the Eagles, I learned that some of the married guys like Chuck Bednarik actually worked second jobs DURING the season. Nobody was playing for the money. I wasn't in the best of shape at that time, but I used my home-town topography to get my legs and wind prepared for camp. Every morning I'd go out and run up the hills, walk down, run up again; a couple of months of this and I was ready for the NFL. I also worked on my punting at my old high school. I was a rarity for the time in that, in addition to working on distance, I would practice angling the ball inside the 20 toward both sidelines. The 'coffin corner' kick wasn't yet used much in professional football, but I always considered myself to be a student of punting. My instincts were correct, but my timing was prematurely off. It wasn't really until a few years later that angled punting inside the 20 became a more commonly deployed strategy in professional football. I guess I was a bit ahead of my time with my 'coffin kicks'. Later when I played with the New York Titans, Sammy Baugh would be one of the first coaches to call for these types of kicks.

I also figured that being able to punt the ball might provide some extra insurance in making the team. It wasn't until the 1960's that punters became specialists who did nothing else but kick the ball, most NFL punters in the '50's were position players who doubled up as punters. I wish I had foreseen the coming specialization of the kicking game, I would have put more focus on that and less on running the ball. If I had spent an hour a day working on my punting, I might have been able to re-establish myself as a full-time punter and possibly added another 10 or 12 years to my career.

I arrived at Hershey for training camp and every morning was a dream for me. We lived in the Hershey Hotel during camp and would have breakfast there, then walk past the amusement park on our way to the stadium. I enjoyed every step of that walk as a professional football player. The park was so colorful and the surrounding countryside was the most perfect shade of green. I still picture that walk in my mind.

I thought I was having a good camp, but sweated it out every day, always waiting for the cut list to go up on the bulletin board. I wasn't sure I was going to make the team until I got the official word from, of all people, my father.

Dad came out to Hershey for a visit near the end of training camp. Our coach, Buck Shaw, was an outgoing and approachable sort, and my father had no reservations about introducing himself and inquiring about my status.

"Is my son gonna make-a the team," he asked, and Buck responded with a thumbs up signal. Dad reported back to me, "No sweat, you're-a in."

I survived training camp and was essentially the sixth running back in the 1959 season. It was a tough backfield to crack. The five backs in front of me had all been with the team for at least one year, and all had impressive college pedigrees. The Eagles used their first two picks in the 1957 draft on running backs: Clarence Peaks, Michigan State, first round and Billy Ray Barnes, Wake Forest, second round. The Eagles also had two other running backs on the roster who had been recent first round selections, Dick Bielski, selected out of Maryland in 1955, and Walt Kowalczyk, taken out of Michigan in 1958. The running back rotation was rounded out by Theron Sapp, who was only a 10th round pick in '58, but had been a two-year starter at Georgia and finished third in the SEC in rushing his senior year. Not an easy rotation to break, all of other runners were credentialed college players, most were high draft picks, and only Bielski, at age 27, was older than me. No exceptional talents, but the backfield was deep and solid.

I was 25 that summer, old for a rookie. In addition to running back, I was also listed as the backup punter and played on all of the special teams. Kickoff returns were especially rough. Pete Retzlaff and I were the outside men in the wedge, just in front of the return men, and we had to block the first guys who came down on the coverage. We both took and delivered a lot of hits. The coverage guys would come flying at you like they were on motorcycles and we took them head on. Pete broke his arm blocking on the wedge that season.

I'm always thankful for having made that team, but I just didn't seem to catch the break that would allow me to distinguish myself. Though I never would have wished injury on anyone, I was somewhat unlucky in that none of the guys ahead of me on the depth chart ever got seriously hurt during my professional career. In the many years since that, I have watched football as a fan and I've seen a number backup guys get their chance because the player in front of him was hurt and they used the opportunity to make a name for themselves. I'd think to myself, "If I had only gotten that chance."

I suited up for every game during the Eagles 9-5 second-place 1959 season, seeing action in seven games. My stat line for the season reads 2 carries for 5 yards and two catches for 9 yards. One crown jewel, black ink achievement does stand out: I led the team in punting average for the season, with 45.0. That does come with an asterisk and, of course with me being me, there is a story attached.

Norm Van Brocklin did all of our punting that year, I was his backup. One game in Washington, it was wet and rainy and Dutch didn't want to go in and kick. We were pinned down on about the five yard line and he turns to me and says, "Hey rook, you take this one, go in and kick." I got off a good kick and pulled us out of the hole. The team stats for the year show, Pagliei, one punt, 45.0 average; Norm Van Brocklin, 53 punts, 42.7 average. I always rubbed that in with Van Brocklin and he'd say to me, "You son of a bitch, one punt and you lead the team."

Dutch was a naturally gifted leader, but more important, he was the force that brought a bunch of great guys even closer together. Dutch made everyone feel like they were part of the team and it worked so well that many of us have remained friends for more than 55 years. There were no cliques within the Eagles, when Dutch got the guys together everyone got an invitation. Hell, Dutch even served as a one-man car pool, driving around to pick guys up. He personally made sure to get as many guys as possible together every Monday morning. It was those Monday sessions that really stand out in my memory. They brought us closer and, I have no doubt, helped make the Eagles the team of destiny they were to become the next season. Some of the most important friendships of my life grew out of my association with the Philadelphia Eagles during that 1959 season.

All of the single guys lived at the Walnut Park Plaza at 63rd and Walnut. Every Monday morning Van Brocklin, who was married and living in the suburbs, would drop his kids off at school and come by the hotel to pick up my roommates, Theron Sapp and Billy Ray Barnes, and me, and we'd would we'd go over to Donahue's to shoot the breeze and drink beer. The other guys would all start drifting in during the morning. This was a very close team, everybody hung together, even in the off-season. Those of us who stayed around Philly would get together, go to the racetrack, play basketball or just hang out. But those Mondays during the season were special: all of us sitting around Donahues, talking football and becoming brothers.

Dutch was an exceptional person. He was always reminding me that I should spend more time with my playbook and less at the pizza parlor because I sometimes had trouble remembering the plays. He was also, physically, about the strongest person I ever met. He must have retired undefeated as the all-time arm wrestling champion. We would go into bars and Dutch would announce, "Anyone want to Indian arm wrestle? Drinks for the bar if I lose." The biggest guy in the place would come over to take him on and Dutch would just about tear the guy's shoulder out of its socket.

We had back-to-back games on the west coast that year. After we played the 49ers in San Francisco, we stayed at a place called Ricky's Studio Inn. The neighborhood kids became aware that the Eagles were staying there and every day a bunch of them with show up with bags full of stuff for us to sign. When they would come up to me and ask who I was and I'd say, "Joe Pagliei," they'd look at me like, "Who?," and keep walking. After a while I got smart and would answer, "Norm Van Brocklin," and then it would be, "Please sign this, Mr. Van Brocklin." I spent that week signing more 'Norm Van Brocklin's' than the Dutchman himself. Dutch got a kick out of that story.

Van Brocklin pretty much ran the offense. Whenever a decision had to be made, Buck Shaw would ask, "What do you think, Dutch?" One game I was wearing the headphones on the field and our offensive coordinator Charlie Gauer was up in the press box. Charlie calls down to me and says, "Joe, hurry up, put Dutch on the phone." I call over to Van Brocklin and he says, "Goddamn it, what the hell does he want now?" He grabs the phone, listens for a few seconds and says, "Yeah, yeah, yeah. What the hell play do you think I've been setting up for?" He goes back on the field and throws a touchdown next play.

Van Brocklin was one of two veteran leaders on that Eagles team. The other was Chuck Bednarik. While Van Brocklin made sure I got to the pub on Monday morning, it was Concrete Charlie who would get me up for church on Sunday. Chuck was no teetotaler, but he was deeply religious and never missed Mass.

One Sunday morning during training camp Chuck comes into my room and says, "Pagliei, you're Italian, right? That means you're Catholic. Get out of bed, you're going to Mass with me." I probably should have been going sooner on my own, but that helped turned me around and it's been part of my life since. I don't close my conversations with good-bye, for me it's always a 'God Bless.'

As I mentioned, Billy Ray Barnes and Theron Sapp were my roommates that year. Theron was a good old boy who loved to sit around, drink wine and talk Georgia football; but he was no simple redneck. He made a ton of money owning and operating a chain of fried chicken restaurants in the South after he retired.

Billy Ray, who had gone to Wake Forest, and I became lifelong friends. He was one of the most colorful people you could ever hope to meet. Billy loved to drink and he was always surrounded by beautiful women. One night we were coming home in his powder blue Cadillac convertible with a couple of women and a cop stopped us on Walnut Street for running a red light. The cop comes over, asks for ID, and when he realizes that he had just stopped Billy Ray Barnes, he says, "Oh, my God; I'm gonna help you out." He ended up letting us go. (Side note: When I saw all the action Billy Ray was getting with that car, I went out and bought a dark blue Cadillac for myself.)

Billy Ray and I still communicate regularly. He's down in Landisville, North Carolina, so we don't see each other as much. We still get together once or twice a year for golf. He could crack a golf ball, but I could usually hit it out there with him. He'd call me a 'Mullet Chunker' and say I couldn't keep up with him. Last time we played he drove the ball about 20 yards past me. I picked up my ball and walked over to him. He said, "What are you doing?" and I said, "Shit, I'm hitting with you." Billy Ray Barnes is just a good, solid, all-around guy. It's because of him that I got into golf, which opened so many opportunities for me later in life. Billy himself got into golf because he got caught up in the Arnold Palmer craze. Arnie, of course, had also gone to Wake Forest though he was a few years ahead of Billy.

One year, Billy went down to Wake Forest to play in their alumni game against the current roster and he invited me to tag along. We get down there and they were short a running back. He asked me if I wanted to suit up and I said, "Hell, yeah," so I played one game as an alumnus of Wake Forest University.

Another year, Billy and I were invited to play at Manufacturers Country Club just outside Philadelphia. We were both hitting the ball lousy all day and the last hole, Billy was so disgusted he picked up his bag and threw it, with all his clubs, into a pond. We start walking to the car, and I asked, "You're not going to leave them there are you?" He said, "Yeah, you're right," and paid some kid to jump into the pond and get them.

Billy Ray Barnes was a second-round draft pick of the Philadelphia Eagles in 1957. He had been an All-American at Wake Forest as well as the ACC Player of the Year. He made the Pro Bowl his first three years in the NFL, and like many of the unmarried Eagles players, lived at the Walnut Street Plaza at 63rd and Walnut in West Philadelphia. Joe Pagliei became a roommate prior to the 1959 season. Billy Ray and Joe have remained close friends, play golf together whenever possible and both report that Billy Ray has refrained from tossing his clubs in the water in recent years. He recalls his friendship with Joe:

"That time at Manufacturers wasn't the only time I threw my clubs in the water, wasn't the first and wasn't the last. I think the last time I tossed my clubs was at an Eagles reunion in Hershey. I tossed the whole bag into the water and was going to leave them, but Maxie Baughan retrieved it for me. I still get together to play golf with Joe and he's become an even better golfer as he's gotten old. Joe's my boy; one of the best people I've ever known. He's a genuine person who would do anything for anybody. If Joe says he's going to do something, it's done.

"He moved in with me at 63rd and Walnut and we had some good times. I can't repeat many of the stories, let's just say we did what young men did at the time. Don't believe any of the rumors you might have heard about me, none of them are true. We ran around together until Joe met Rita, and with that his life changed for the better. They are the perfect couple. I remember when he met her and I remember driving up from North Carolina through as snowstorm to get to their wedding. They remain today, two of the best people.

"West Philly was a hell of a nice place to live back then, I fell in love with the city and I still consider Philly to be my home. I still love cheesesteaks. We used to get a Craps game going in our apartment and we'd order the best cheesesteaks from a place on 62nd and Market. I could hear the guy on the other end of the phone groan whenever I'd ask for mayonnaise on mine. He'd say, "Sounds like you guys are having one of your Craps games."

These were the Philadelphia Eagles that I was part of and I was looking forward to the 1960 season. Training camp opened in Hershey on July 24; expectations were high: new decade, new confidence. The team yearbook offered the following pre-season summary:

"The outlook for 1960 is quite bright thanks to a major overhaul in 1959 that brought the team from last place to a tie for second. A total of 18 new players, including 11 rookies, spiced the 1959 squad to a record of seven won and five lost as against a log of 2-9-1 in 1958. A sound nucleus of returnees will form the backbone of the 1960 Eagles plus a generous sprinkling of new men."

Entering my second training camp, I was feeling like a veteran. We lost one running back during the off season, Dick Bielski had been left unprotected in the expansion draft and was taken by the newly formed Dallas Cowboys. The Eagles did, however, draft another running back in the first round of the draft. This time it was

Ron Burton of Northwestern. But this was also the first season of the new American Football League and Burton elected to sign with the Boston Patriots who had also drafted him. One rookie running back who was drafted did show up for training camp, Ted Dean, taken in the fourth round from Wichita State.

Another new face in the backfield was Timmy Brown, who had been drafted by the Green Bay Packers in the 27th round in 1959 and cut during the season. He joined the Eagles as a free agent shortly after training camp started in 1960.

So, my competition entering the season were three returning backs, Billy Ray Barnes, Clarence Peaks and Theron Sapp; rookie draft pick Ted Dean and free agent addition Tim Brown.

I was nervous, as coaches indicated that they were only going to carry five running backs during the season.

Eddie Khayat played defensive end for the Eagles from 1958-61 and coached the team 1971-72. He was a teammate of Joe Pagliei in 1959 and during the 1960 preseason training camp:

"Joe was a really good player; he was tough and didn't back down from anybody. One practice he got a little too aggressive and cut me down below the knee. The Swamp Fox (Marion Campbell) jumped in Joe's face while I was down on the ground, giving him hell for throwing a block like that in practice. Joe stood his ground and gave it right back to Marion."

The Eagles were scheduled to open the regular season at home, September 23, hosting the Cleveland Browns. On September 19, they announced their final cuts. The last man to be let go was one Joe Pagliei.

I was leaving practice at the University of Pennsylvania and got to the end of the driveway when general manager Vince McNally called me back. He acknowledged that they might be making a mistake, but they were still letting me go. The day they cut me was picture day; they didn't announce the last cut until after the team picture was taken, so I can be found in the team photo of the 1960 NFL Champions.

I was the last cut in 1960, the Wednesday before the first game. That really sucked and I've always believed that it was as much for budget reasons as anything else. The team ended up carrying one player less than the roster allotment for the whole season.

Billy Ray Barnes was both surprised and saddened the day his friend and roommate was released from the team. He thought Joe had acquitted himself well and had earned a spot on the roster:

"Joe was a tough, tough son-of-a-gun. He could do it all on the football field; he was a good runner, played on all the special teams and had an unbelievable leg. He could punt, kick field goals, kick off. He was a good football player. He was always stocky, weighed about 225, and was strong and fast. it was a matter of numbers, we were carrying five running backs and I guess the last spot came

down to Joe and Theron Sapp. Then, right after that, Theron got hurt and I was hoping that they would call Joe back, but by that time he had already signed with the AFL."

Eddie Khayat also recalls the logjam at running back going into the 1960 season and the injury to Theron Sapp:

"It was all numbers. Ted Dean came in as a rookie and he was a terrific player for us that year. Sapp and Barnes and Peaks were all proven veterans. I remember when Sapp got hurt, he was down on the field yelling for Billy Ray to come in and take his place. Billy Ray thought he was tired and was trying to get a blow, and yelled back, "Let him go, leave him in there, he's just tired." Except for Theron, we stayed healthy most of the year. Later in the season, Clarence got hurt and by that time Theron was ready to come back. Joe missed out because he had already signed with the Titans."

That 1960 Eagles team still holds a very dear place in the hearts and minds of Philadelphia sports fans. It remains today, the last Eagles team to win an NFL championship. The members of that team have been feted on a number of occasions through the years. I may not have made the roster or played a single down that season, but I am blessed to have left enough of an impression on my teammates that I have been included in every one of the reunions.

I'm so grateful to be recognized as an 'honorary member' of the 1960 NFL Championship team. The guys have never forgotten me and this has helped taken some sting out of the dubious distinction of being the final cut of a championship team. It was tough leaving the Eagles, there was so much camaraderie.

I miss so many of those guys who are gone: Bob Pellegrini, Jesse Richardson, Tom Brookshier. Jesse was the best man at my wedding and he was the one who first got me going to go to the racetrack. That whole team was all good people, there wasn't a single guy that nobody liked. I was only with the Eagles for year, but I made lifelong friends. Tommy McDonald became my best friend: I'm godfather to his daughter Tish and his wife Patty is godmother to one of my kids. When we were moving to Atlantic City from Pennsauken because of my casino job, I bought a new house before we had sold the one we were living in and I was about $20,000 short of the down payment. One night Tommy and his wife Patty were having dinner with Rita and me. I told them about the new house and that we were trying to figure out how to make it work as we wouldn't have the full deposit until we sold our present house. Neither of them said anything, but the next week Tommy and Patty came back to visit and Patty handed me a check for $20,000 and said not to worry about anything until we sold our house. When we sold our house, I made out two checks, one for $20,000 and another for $1,500 and told them the other check was our way of saying thanks and we wanted them to use it to do something for their kids. They tore up the second check, said they wouldn't hear of it.

We've always stayed close as couples, Rita and Patty get along very well. Meeting in Chinatown for dinner, we'd come from New Jersey and I'd park my car on the street, then you'd see Tommy and Patty come flying into town on Tommy's motorcycle. Patty would be holding on in the back and Tommy would always find a spot to park the motorcycle right in front of the restaurant. When we'd go out to visit them at their house in King of Prussia, Tommy would put on a show doing stunts on his motorcycle. He'd stand on the seat or drive down a hill without touching the handlebars.

Now, Tommy suffers from Alzheimer's and other ailments and Patty has Parkinson's Disease. They are a beautiful couple and it breaks our hearts to see them this way now. We were at an Eagles alumni function in 2015 when they announced us in alphabetical order and Tommy and I were standing on the field together. Mike Mamula was standing with us and he asked Tommy what he remembered about his playing days, Tommy looked at him with a blank stare and said, "Nothing."

Bob Pellegrini remained one of my closest friends. He and I started working in Atlantic City together and he was also responsible for me getting one of my most memorable part-time gigs. I was scuffling for a buck after Garden State Racetrack burned down and I lost my job as a jockey agent. Pelly called me one day asked if I wanted to be a bodyguard for Tom Jones, who was going to be in Philly for an appearance at The Spectrum. A local guy we knew from the racetrack, Peter DePaul, was promoting the event and was also a big horseman. He told Pelly that he would pay us each $100 a day to shadow Jones and just hang out with him. Jones was a great guy. We were with him in the dressing room and got to walk him out to the stage. One woman got so excited that she tried to jump at him and give him a hug. I got between them and the crazed woman tore my suit trying to get at him. It was brand-new suit and had cost me about $100, which was good money in those days.

Jim "Gummy" Carr was another great teammate. He was a defensive back from West Virginia. Boy could he hit, but he was also the nicest, goofiest guy; everybody liked him. He was also, shall we say, the best endowed guy any of us had ever been around and he put everybody to shame in the shower. I went up to his wife Lila one time and said, "I have to shake your hand and congratulate you for living with Gummy." She knew what I was talking about and laughed.

Sonny Jurgensen lived in the same hotel with us and he was another good guy. He had been a starter before the team brought Van Brocklin in, but he never complained. I think at that stage of his career, Sonny thought he just wasn't good enough to play quarterback in the NFL. Of course he went to make the Hall of Fame, mostly as a result of his years with the Redskins, but at that time he was content to watch and learn from Van Brocklin. Sonny and I signed our contracts the same day; we each got a $500 bonus and were thrilled because that was big money.

My favorite person from that team was Jesse Richardson. He was the best man at my wedding, that's how special he was to me. We used to go the racetrack together, smoke cigars and have a good time. For a big guy, he always had a gorgeous woman on his arm. There was this one, Monica Mayo, and I remember she broke up with him by phone while we were on the road and he just hung up the phone and said, "Oh, well." Jesse was as unfazed as a just-dumped guy could be. He always had a backup inventory of women that he could move on to.

Eddie Khayat and I also became friends from that team. We were up in New York and I went out to buy some shirts when I bumped into Buck Shaw in the men's room and he asked, "What are you up to, boy?" I told him I was shopping and had bought about a dozen shirts. I told Eddie the story, he started laughing and my nickname from Eddie became 'Shirts.' We stay in touch and I still go out to his charity golf outing in York every year.

Eddie Khayat has a somewhat different recollection of the origin of the nickname:

"Dutch (Norm Van Brocklin) started calling Joe 'Shirts'. Dutch was the one who gave out all of the nicknames and we picked up on them. Joe came back from shopping all excited about a sale on shirts that he found. He liked the style so much that he bought one of every color. Dutch wasn't about to let something like that go, whenever he saw Joe, he'd yell over, 'Hey, Shirts', or ask him if that was one of his new shirts that he was wearing."

Everybody on that Eagles team knew how to have a good time and Tom Brookshier was at the top of that list. Most of America got to know him when he was part of the NFL's number one broadcast team with Pat Summerall. He was as tough a defensive back as there was in the league and he never cheated himself out of a good time off the field. One night, Brookie, Billy Barnes and I were going to a club on 66th Street. We see a shopping cart on the sidewalk and we stuffed Brookie into it. I opened the doors to the club and Billy Ray pushed the cart in with Brookie sitting in it waving to everyone. Everybody in the club knew who he was and went wild when they saw him buzzing through the crowd in that cart.

I can't emphasize enough what a nice bunch of guys they were. It means everything to me that I'm recognized as an honorary member of the 1960 championship team. Football didn't end for me that year, as I headed up to New York, but there was no way that I could replicate the memories and friendships that I'm blessed to have made as a Philadelphia Eagle.

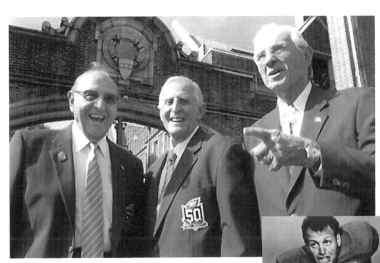

Tommy McDonald (center), Chuck
Bednarik (right) and myself at
Franklin Field in Philadelphia being
honored for the 1960 Philadelphia
Eagles Championship.

THE PHILADELPHIA EAGLES

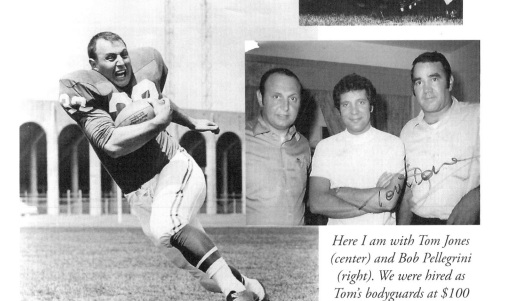

Here I am with Tom Jones
(center) and Bob Pellegrini
(right). We were hired as
Tom's bodyguards at $100
for two nights.

JOE PAGLIEI, HB   6'0"   220 lbs.   Clemson

5 – NEW YORK TITANS

I was devastated by the cut from the Eagles and in some ways still haven't recovered. I can only say it so many times and so many ways, but that Eagles team was the best group of people I was ever associated with. Add to it the fact that I've continued to live in the Philadelphia area and that the 1960 team remains, to this day, the only Eagles team to win a championship in nearly 70 years, and that's part of my legacy, last guy cut by a team that goes on to win a championship. A stunning blow, but I did not remain unemployed for long. By the time I returned to my room at the Walnut Park Plaza, messages were waiting from three or four teams in the brand-new American Football League. The most urgent of these messages was from the Denver Broncos. Like most people, I knew very little about the Broncos or any of the other seven teams in this new league.

One thing that I did know about the Broncos was that they were getting attention for what might be the ugliest uniforms anyone had ever seen. The primary colors were yellow, black and brown, with both the yellow and white jersey accented by vertically striped socks that would long live in infamy. The white jerseys were accompanied by socks with brown and white stripes running up and down the lower leg; the yellow jersey, which in and of itself was painful to look at, was worn with brown and yellow vertically striped socks. The story behind the uniforms is that the Broncos general manager allegedly bought them at a fire sale auction when the Copper Bowl went out of business.

Those socks. They wanted to me to come in and start punting for them on Sunday, but I couldn't go out there because I didn't want to be anywhere near those damned socks. I couldn't get them out of my mind. People thought I was nuts: an unemployed football player turning down a job offer because of the socks. I'm sure I'm one of the few guys in the history of professional sports who rejected a team because he didn't like the uniforms. What can I say, I've always been picky about the way I dressed.

The next call I returned was from Steve Sebo of the New York Titans. Sebo had previously been the head coach at the University of Pennsylvania which shared its home stadium, Franklin Field, with the Eagles. Sebo was now general manager of the Titans and his team was in need of a punter. He saw the name Joe Pagliei on the cut list and remembered watching me boom the ball at Franklin Field.

I went up to New York and it turned out to be one of the most memorable days of my life. I signed a contract on the spot and got a 25% raise. I walk out of the Titans office in the Manhattan Hotel feeling pretty good about things, stop in for a drink at a bar across the street and I meet Lauren Bacall. She was sitting at the bar and I immediately recognized her; up to that point in my life Lauren Bacall remains the second prettiest woman I had ever seen, right behind Rita. We started talking and she told me to call her Betty. I was telling her I had just signed a contract with the New York Titans and, like most people in New York, she didn't know what the hell the Titans were. She was very nice and told some stories about Humphrey Bogart and other Hollywood people. I was about to get up to leave and she said to stick around, Jason Robards was coming to meet her. After a while Jason Robards comes in and we all sat around having drinks. What a way to cap off a nice day. She was a beautiful woman and my number one actress, ever.

In signing with the Titans, I'm now a member of my third different professional football league in five years. That had to make me one of, if not the first, to complete the trifecta of playing in the Canadian Football League, National Football League and the American Football League. Add in those two years of Army ball, and I wore four different uniforms between 1957 and 1960. I didn't care; I just wanted to play football.

The increase in pay was appreciated, but I quickly learned that it also came with some strings attached. Specifically, some of those paychecks were made of rubber. The whole Titans organization was completely unorganized and checks started bouncing early on. Sammy Baugh, the head coach, felt bad when the checks started going bad, he gave me $500 out of his own pocket.

Joe Pagliei and Rita DiPasquale became engaged to be married in October of 1960. Rita well recalls the financial uncertainty that accompanied being a member of the nascent Titans:

"There was one payday where the team was leaving for a game in California the next day. Joe gave me his paycheck and told me deposit in the bank immediately, IMMEDIATELY. I asked him why and he said that he wanted to make sure the money was there to cover the check."

We didn't have any team doctors. Early in the season, when we were playing in Houston, a guard named Howard Glenn broke his neck on a play and was down on the field. He was taken to the hospital after the game and while we were waiting for him at the airport for the flight back to New York, we found out that he had died. We land in New York and apparently the news is carrying reports that a Titans player died during the game. Rita and I were engaged at the time and her mother heard on the television that a Titan player had just died and got her worried. Rita couldn't reach me because we were already in the air. As soon as the plane landed I called to let her know I was okay.

It took the death of Glenn for the AFL to mandate that all teams had to have doctors on their sidelines and each stadium needed to be equipped with x-ray equipment.

I continued to live in Philadelphia while playing in New York and had more contact with my former Eagles teammates than I did with the Titans. That was a rough year for me, watching a championship season unfurl when I had been so close to being part of it. I hung out with the guys at the hotel and even went to a couple of Eagles games when my schedule allowed.

I commuted to New York with Jim Katcavage and Eddie Bell, who were both playing for the Giants. We'd take a 7 am train from Philly to New York every morning. I'd go to the Polo Grounds, they'd go to Yankee Stadium. Practice started at 9:30, 12:30 we'd be back on the train to Philly.

The Polo Grounds was a dump. The stadium had barely been used since the baseball Giants left in 1957. There was brown stuff coming out of the showers, backed up toilets, rusty lockers and bad odors. I don't think I ever got comfortable with the Titans and it was tough for me watching what was going on with the Eagles. Something special was building, the city was getting more excited every week and all my friends were part of it. I'd see the guys during the week: they were winning and having a ball while I'm playing in a landfill of a stadium with paychecks bouncing all over the place.

What made the separation even tougher was that the Eagles did offer me the opportunity to return to the team when they realized that Theron Sapp was hurt worse than they thought and would not be returning as anticipated. They asked me if I was interested in coming back, but I had already signed a contract with the Titans. That really stung; I missed those guys. There was so much camaraderie with that team.

I didn't know anything about the AFL. All I knew was that this guy, Lamar Hunt, said he would make sure the league had enough money to last for 10 years. I just took the job; I was getting married after the season and needed the paycheck. Harry Wismer, the owner of the Titans, was a nice guy, a real character and always running around with one of Franklin Roosevelt's sons, but everything about the Titans was so shaky. The Roosevelt son used to wear one of those long coats like his father and he would stand on the sidelines with Wismer while Harry would be telling us that we were better than the Giants and we would crush them right now if they played us.

Harry Wismer was never low-key about anything, he always wanted to make sure his presence was known. One night he was invited to a big fight in Philadelphia, he couldn't make it but the told the announcers to say that he was right there at ringside. With his background in radio and television, Harry understood the importance of broadcasting. He hired Les Keiter to do our games. Keiter was a big time announcer and he always gave me a plug; whenever I set up to punt he would spell out my name "P-A-G-L-I-E-I."

Harry was also one of the founders of the AFL and he saw the opportunity to do something special with a team in New York. In selecting the name 'Titans' he explained, "Titans are bigger and stronger than Giants." The New York Giants played in Yankee Stadium, right across the East River from us, and Harry took aim at them as soon as he got his franchise. Unlike some of the other charter owners, he did not come into football with deep pockets and was always struggling to keep the team afloat. I saw an article in the Star-Ledger newspaper around 2007, where linebacker Larry Grantham said that coaches used to keep us running extra laps on paydays so that they, the coaches, could "jump into their cars and get to the bank first." That pretty much summed up that first season with the New York Titans.

Harry was instrumental, if not the key figure, in orchestrating the AFL's first television contract. He himself had been a broadcaster for 20 years and had connections to high level people at the American Broadcasting Company. ABC carried us locally in New York and there were national games on the network every week. The money from that early television contract, I have to believe, kept a lot of AFL afloat. It was Harry who helped develop the concept that the league's overall television revenue would be shared equally among all the teams. This plan would serve as the model that exists today for the television contracts of the National Football League.

Things were so minor league with the Titans that first year that I ended up buying my own football helmet. I get to New York and my second or third day there they put me in a scrimmage and tell me to run the ball. They had given me this little MacGregor helmet. Everybody on defense is waiting for me and I run a draw play. Larry Grantham comes over the top of the center and knocks me back, I hit my head and it knocks me cuckoo. Of course there were no team doctors on the sideline and my head hurt. The next day I called Riddell and ordered my own helmet. The day it gets delivered I bring it with me to practice and tell them I'm not wearing that MacGregor any more. The new helmet was white, so I give it to Nick the ballboy and he did a real shitty job of painting it. He spray-painted it black with a yellow stripe down the top. At least I felt safe. One of my daughters still has that helmet and today it's a collector's item. We were offered money for it a couple of times: one guy offered $700 and a few years later another guy offered $1500.

Larry Grantham may have been the best player on that team. He had been drafted by the Titans in 1960 from the University of Mississippi. I still stay involved with the Jets alumni association and they do a good job of remembering the old Titans. Larry was one of three original Titans, along with receiver Don Maynard and running back Bill Mathis, who would still be with the franchise when the New York Jets won the Super Bowl in 1969. Those three were also among only 20 players who were in the AFL for its entire 10-year existence and the seven who stayed with the same franchise during that time.

Larry wasn't very big, but he could hit. He basically knocked me into getting a new helmet. I remember another one of his hits that we still talk about: we were playing Oakland and they had a big running back come out of the backfield. Larry comes up and meets him and literally took him right out of his pants. We were all laughing, they had to stop the game so this guy could put his pants back on. Oakland was probably like most teams in the league, they had all the uniforms in a pile, a guy comes in and the equipment guy tosses him a pair of pants. None of us wore anything that was fitted.

Head coach Sammy Baugh, was a true NFL legend as a player. He would become one the inductees into the Pro Football Hall of Fame's 17-man charter class of 1963. He coached the Titans for their first two seasons of existence and had record of 14-14. He won two NFL championships as quarterback for the Washington Redskins. In 1943, he had what may be the greatest all-around season by a player in NFL history. As quarterback he led the league in passing and as a defensive back he led the league with 11 interceptions while also having the highest punting average in the league at

45.9 yards. He led the league in punting from 1940-43, still has the second best career average in NFL history (45.1) and his 51.4 average in 1940 remains the best single season in league history.

For me, the punter on that first Titans team, it was an honor to practice kicks with Sammy Baugh. We used to line up opposite each other and kick back and forth. After each kick we would move back three steps to see who could kick the longest. He was about 42 years old and he still beat me every time. He could look one way, kick the ball the other way and get a great punt off every time. Sammy taught me a lot about punting. He was one of the first coaches to emphasize angle kicking; kicking out of bounds inside the 20. My punting average that year was about 37 yards. It could have been higher, but I gave up yards angling balls toward the sideline. He taught me to kick away from the return man. If we had kept the elaborate statistics they do today, I'd probably be right near the top in fewest average yards per return. I was the league leader in punting for a few weeks, but lost some yardage because Sammy had me kicking the ball out of bounds.

I finished that inaugural season of the American Football League averaging 37.1 yards per punt. Paul Maguire of the Buffalo Bills, who later became a popular NFL color commentator, led the league with 40.1. My 48 total punts ranked seventh.

My stat line for 1960 includes 17 rushes for 69 yards with a long run of 25 yards and one touchdown. I also caught one pass for 13 yards.

In May of 1959, I met Rita DiPasquale at a dance at the Drexelbrook Club in West Philadelphia. As Rita recalls, it was not the one most romantic of first encounters, but less than nine months later we would be married.

Rita Pagliei remains today spry and attractive, there can be little doubt why Joe was attracted to her. She is one of those people who have been blessed since middle age to look at least 20 years less than her actual age. While the courtship was quick, Joe's opening line was less than gallant. A native of West Philadelphia, Rita was an undergraduate student at the University of Pennsylvania when she first met Joe:

"I was at the dance with a friend of mine, Joan, who was a tall blond and was wearing a fitted dress. I was wearing a pleated skirt and looked like I had just come from class. Joe was after my friend all night. Joe was there with Billy Ray Barnes and Joan went off with Billy. Joe comes up and says, 'Looks like I'm stuck with you'. My first reaction was 'uhh'. I was a student at an Ivy League school and he's wearing a silk Italian suit with a teardrop pattern. Joe and I started dancing while Joan and Billy were sitting at a table. Every time I looked over at Billy, he was avoiding me.

"It was decided that it was easier for her to take Billy home because he was living in a hotel near 30th Street Station and Joan was headed that way. Joe drove me. We stopped at a diner and when we pulled in front of my house he said, 'How about going out with me tomorrow night?' I told him that I didn't know because

I was seeing another guy at the time, but I gave him my phone number and told him to call me. We were parked in front of my house and it was about two in the morning. The light on my front porch was flicking off and on, off and on. Joe asked what that was about and I told him it must be a short, but I knew it was my mother telling me to get my butt in the house. Joe walked me to the front door and my parents came out in their pajamas. They were very little people and my mother was wearing mismatched pajamas, a plaid top with zebra bottoms. My father, a little man, gets in Joes face and tells him, 'Do you know what time it is? My daughter is a nice girl, don't let this happen again'.

I was 22, and my mother and father were still waiting up for me. I was expected home by 12:30."

We became engaged in October midway through the 1960 season. I was living in the basement of the DiPasquale home and commuting from 30th Street Station to the Polo Grounds.

Rita recalls Joe's move from the Walnut Plaza to her parent's basement:
"Joe was telling my mother and me that it was really depressing being around all of the Eagles and not being part of the team. Of course my sweet mother told him that he could stay in our basement. Joe lit up. The basement was finished and very cozy. Joe was very comfortable there."

Rita and her girlfriend Joan used to come up to New York for the Titans' home games. She was always taken aback and commented on how shocked she was that there were so few people at a professional football game.

We were married in January 1961 at St. Donato Church. Philadelphia was hit with a 16-inch snow storm the day before the wedding. Rita's uncle, Clarence Ferguson, who was a captain with the Philadelphia police vice squad, was able to call in a favor and a city-owned snow plow was dispensed to clean the streets around the church to accommodate our guests. Unfortunately for me, it was right around the time of the wedding that I was notified by the Titans that I was not going to be brought back for the 1961 season.

Rita was appreciative of her uncle's efforts to get the roads cleared for the wedding:
"Joe insisted on getting married that winter and we got sixteen inches of snow the day before our wedding. I was worried about the snow and our guests being able to get to the wedding. It took only a phone call from Uncle Clarence to get the city snow plows to clear a path to the roads leading to the church. My uncle, Clarence Ferguson, was a detective captain and the head of the vice squad in Philadelphia. He was a big mean-looking man; looked like a football player. He arrested a lot of junkies around town and made a name for himself as the detective who arrested Billie Holiday on drug charges at her hotel in Philadelphia."

I didn't get any offers that winter, but did hook up with the Buffalo Bills just as training camp was starting. In looking back, I have to admit that I never stood a chance to make the team. I got a call from Buster Ramsey who was head coach of the Bills. He said Cookie Gilchrist just got hurt and he needed a fullback. He asked me if I was in shape, I said, "Are you kidding?" So he said, "Get your ass up here" and he sent me a plane ticket.

I get up there on Wednesday and on Sunday he starts me. First play I get about seven yards, next play about 10 yards. Then they throw me a screen pass and I go for about 25 yards. Next thing I'm leaning on a fence and waving for them to send a replacement in. Ramsey gets ahold of me and says, "You lied to me you son-of-a-bitch, you're not in shape" and they sent me home. After that I went to the Hamilton Tiger Cats for a little while, but that didn't last. If I have known how great the NFL was going to be I would have taken better care of myself.

I don't know why it happened, but I allowed myself to get completely out of shape that off-season. There was no such thing as off-season workouts in those days, but it seems like I didn't do anything but eat after I got married. I wish now that I had taken football more seriously and took better care of myself. I know I could have played a few more years, probably could have hung around as a punter and played another 10-12 years. I've become friendly with Sean Landetta through the Eagles Alumni Association. He lasted more than 20 years in the NFL, just punting the ball. I showed up at the Bills' camp in the worst shape of my life. It's a shame. I loved football, but may have taken it for granted. I should have treated it as my career and worked out more. That off-season I swelled up from 220 to about 250 pounds. I was really heavy.

Rita recalls that Joe didn't work out at all and put on quite a bit of weight as a happy newlywed:

"He looked like Porky Pig, but I have to tell you, his mother loved the way he looked. She'd say, 'Joey, I like you this way, this is how I like to see you', as she was squeezing his double chin and he was splitting his pants. He got as fat as a cow. I was pregnant and he ate like he was having a baby. My mom said, 'Shouldn't he be working out before camp?' He was so out of shape. After he got cut, he laid around on the couch for about two months. Finally my father told him, okay, it's time get up and do something. He took a job selling dictionaries. We really didn't talk about his being cut. Of course I wanted to say, 'Why didn't you listen to me and not put on so much weight?' Now he keeps himself in great shape; if he had done it 60 years ago..."

Joe's playing career may have come to an end following the 1960 season, before any of his children were born, but he never really left the game and football was always part of his family life according to daughter Patti:

"Dad had already finished his football career by the time us kids came along,

but the NFL was always such a huge part of our lives growing up because dad never really left. He became really involved with the alumni association. He kept in close contact with friends, players and coaches through the years and we always had visits from notable players. I didn't think that much about football back then, but I loved playing with dad's old helmet and pads."

In her travels with Joe, Rita has seen one too many former professional football players who have grown old before their time as they deal with debilitating mental or physical ailments. At 83 years of age Joe remains both sharp and active. She looks at him with appreciation as she thinks of former teammates who are no longer here or are not able to get up and enjoy life as Joe does every day:

"If anything good happened because of having a short career, it's that he's not paying for it today."

Note: Harry Wismer limped along with the Titans until November 1962 when the other AFL owners took over financial control of the team for the remainder of that season. In early 1963, a group of investors led by Sonny Werblin purchased the team and instituted wholesale changes. The name was changed to Jets, team colors went from blue and gold to green and white, and Weeb Ewbank was named head coach. In 1964 the team moved from the rundown Polo Grounds to the brand-new Shea Stadium. In 1965, with the first pick in the draft they selected quarterback Joe Namath out of the University of Alabama and awarded him with the then unheard of contract of $427,000. In 1969, Ewbank would lead the Jets past his former team, the Baltimore Colts, in Super Bowl III, thus legitimizing the AFL as a professional football entity.

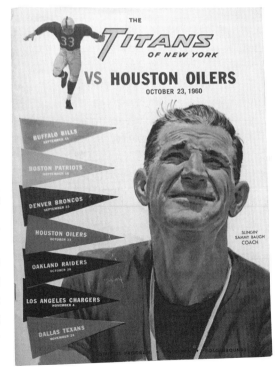

I like to think I played a very minor role in helping Namath get to New York. I got a call from one of the Jets front office guys asking me to help them out and go take a look at this quarterback. A few of the guys still felt bad that they had cut me and stayed in touch. I went to the game and was in awe of what I saw. My scouting report simply said something to the effect that Joe Namath was best-looking young guy I had seen at that position in a long time.

6 – JOCKEY AGENT

Those two years I spent in pro football with the Eagles and the Jets would serve me well in my post-football careers. Having played in Philadelphia and New York comes in especially useful if you're carving out a living in New Jersey. I had the fans on both sides of the Delaware and Hudson Rivers covered.

I was involved mostly in sales, some cars, some real estate, and was scrambling to make a living. I did spend as much free time as possible following the ponies. When I was with the Eagles, I started going to the racetrack nearly every day in the off-season with my old teammate, and best man at my wedding, Jesse Richardson. We would show up at one of the Philly-area tracks with The Racing Form under our arms and big cigars in our mouths. At worst, we usually broke even. I was becoming a regular fixture around the tracks and became friendly with a trainer at Keystone named Max Clark. Football was a bond between Max and me. We were both running backs who had good college careers and then played some in the pros. Max was drafted by the Cleveland Browns in 1951 and spent some time on their roster. With our common football backgrounds he took a liking to me. I picked up some good insider strategies that could be applied in the evaluation of horses by hanging around with Max. I had developed an interest in horse racing when my father used to take me to the tracks in West Virginia when I was a kid in Clairton. Under Max's tutelage I was becoming pretty good at picking horses and one day, about 1970, he said to me, "Joe, you should consider getting a job at the track; you'd make a good jockey agent."

I was selling cars at the time and, while I was good at that, car showrooms didn't provide anywhere near the adrenaline rush of the racetrack. One thing I did pick up in the car business was that it was good to wear my Philadelphia Eagles polo shirts or blazer around the showroom. Unlike today, where everybody wears team logo clothing, it was rare to see someone dressed like that. Even then, people loved to talk about their Eagles and my clothing drew them in. When they learned that I was an ex-player, I became their guy. If they're going to buy a car, it's going to be from me. Football always served as a launching platform to get me from one place to another. Even though I didn't have the greatest career, people always seemed to have an appreciation for the fact that I did make it.

Rita Pagliei was for a time concerned about Joe spending so much time at the racetrack while he was selling cars, but became less skeptical as his sales increased in proportion to time spent at Garden State:

"He (Joe) was selling Pontiacs on Admiral Wilson Boulevard. The first year he made about $7,000, which was nothing. The next year he started putting pictures up around his desk of him in his football uniforms and began wearing clothes with Eagles logos to work. He doubled his money and made $14,000 that year. At that time you couldn't buy Eagles paraphernalia anywhere. Joe had some hats and 'Property of the Eagles' t-shirts that he got from the team. You couldn't get that stuff in the stores. Joe would call a customer over and tell him in a low voice, 'Hey buddy, I have a nice t-shirt for you' and they ate it up. He was doing very well

selling cars, and then when Garden State opened up, he was going over there every day. I knew he was betting, but he'd say, 'No, I'm working'. His boss told him that he should be spending more time in the office. Joe insisted that he was selling cars at the track. He would talk to everybody when he was at the track, and he WAS selling cars. Once he proved this, his boss told him, 'Okay, do what you want'. I'd tell him that he should be spending more time at the office, but he'd say the boss told him it was alright. He was very successful selling cars at the track and he was spending so much time there that he said, 'I want to be a jockey agent'."

I loved being around the Garden State track and was successful as a jockey agent right out of the gate. I had a knack for matching jockeys with horses and I would go on to represent some guys who had very nice careers. Although, if I could have done a better job with one wannabe jockey, the streets of Philadelphia might have been a little less bloody and the headlines a bit more tame in the 1980's and 90's, but more about that one later.

Joe Pagliei got into horse racing and later the casino business not by design, but on the recommendations of friends. His son, Joe Jr., would follow in his father's career footsteps in an opposite order, first the casinos and later racing. He is now a successful executive with the Stronach Group, one of the world's leading racetrack operators and suppliers of parimutuel wagering technology. They operate some of the nation's top tracks, including Santa Anita Park, Pimlico Race Course and Gulfstream Park. He recalls the early impressions that were made as he tagged along with his father when Joe Sr., was a jockey agent at Garden State:

"I started going to the horses when I was about six-years old. My dad seemed like he knew everybody. We'd walk around as the horses got ready in the morning for the races in the afternoon. It always seemed like there was so much money around. One of the first jockeys my dad represented was Carlos Lopez, and he was a real character. He used to con the trainers into giving him rides and he was a real wild character, especially with the women. It seemed like he had women and kids all over the place, it was just crazy. He had stories about all of his women and the kids he seemed to have everywhere. He was one of the top jockeys when he put his head into it; but sometimes he would work in the mornings, sometimes he didn't.

"I was reading the Racing Form when I was really young. I helped my dad with his charts, the overnights and the statistics. He kept records on everything, but the best lesson I learned from my dad was how to deal with people. He was always very outgoing; he had something to talk about with everyone, from the guys who were sweeping the stables to the trainers and owners. A lot of people don't have those skills, when he talked to someone, he really talked with them. He would ask questions and try to establish some kind of contact: for instance, if someone said they were from Harrisburg, my dad would bring up the name of restaurant from there. He'd mention something like he had had a great meal at John's Café. He tried to make everyone comfortable."

Max Clark and some others helped me get hooked up with a struggling jockey, John Kevin Daley. Because he wasn't considered to be a strong rider none of the agents wanted to touch him. The job of the jockey agent is to find mounts for their riders and Daley had not earned the confidence of any of them. I approached one of the trainers at Keystone Racetrack, Gordon Potter, about putting Daley on some his horses. Potter was blunt, he told me, "That kid's a shit sack, but I'll find a few horses for him."

The first week I brought Daley out to Keystone, he raced five horses, three of them won. Not a bad introduction for both of us.

I learned to hone in on the better trainers and owners, and I kept notes on everything, a habit that would later serve me well in the casino business. Anytime a trainer or owner would mention anything about jockey or a horse, I'd write the info down, go home, study the notes, do some homework and try to create the best matchups possible.

Probably the most successful horse I was ever associated with was a mare, Dainty Dotsie, who was owned by J.R. Cowden and was trained by his son. She won her debut at Keystone by 17 lengths in December 1976, and she probably won about nine times with one of my jocks riding her. She would win all but one her races during her three-year old season, including a big upset victory at Aqueduct in New York. I always bet on Dotsie, so in addition to getting my 25% commission for supplying the winning jockey, I also cashed in quite a few winning tickets.

I later had another jockey, Billy Phelps, on Dotsie. He won three stakes in a row. After the final race, Phelps got into an argument with Jimmy Cowden, the trainer. Cowden told Phelps that he would never ride another horse for him again. Billy told him to stuff it and that he didn't want to ride for the Cowdens anymore, anyway. There was a big stakes race coming up in two weeks and Dainty Dotsie was entered without rider. I asked Billy Phelps if he would like to ride Dotsie in that race. He said, "You're damned right I'd like ride that horse, but I can't stand Cowden." I told him to leave it to me, I'd fix things up. I went over to Jimmy Cowden and told him that Billy really wanted to make things right. Jimmy said, "Does he really want to? Nobody rides Dotsie like Billy." Cowden made me a deal. He had just gotten his pilot's license and if I agreed to go up and fly with him for 20 minutes, he'd let Billy Phelps ride his horse. That was easy enough for me to agree to. We got on the plane at Northeast Philadelphia Airport, not far from Philadelphia Park. We flew over the Garden State track in Cherry Hill and on the way back it started raining like hell. The sky is getting dark and I asked Jimmy where the hell the ground was; I really wanted to know when this was going to be over and hopefully we would be walking away from the plane. His answer wasn't too reassuring, "Shit, I don't know." Since I'm telling this story, it's obvious we made it back to the airport, but I was never so happy to have my feet touch the ground. That got Billy back on Dainty Dotsie, and together they went on to win six or seven races in row. Billy and Jimmy were now friends again.

Every day at the track I was reminded that most of the people who worked there, jockeys, trainers, grooms and even some of the owners, never even graduated high school and weren't the most intellectual of people. They were street smart, but not deep thinkers. I was always figuring out strategies that would appeal to these people. I was constantly doing things to get rides for my guys and would go above and beyond to ingratiate myself with the trainers. I was always buying drinks, dinners, getting their cars washed, you name it. My mind never stopped operating when I was at the race-track. I was all over the place and everyone liked me. I made it my business to stay away from trouble with any of the trainers or owners.

I used to play cards with a group of guys at Garden State. A favorite game was Racehorse Rummy. Every day after giving the horses a morning workout, we'd go into the track secretary's office and play cards. It was big-assed office with about 10 or 12 guys taking entries from all over the place.

These card games took place at midday, after the morning work was finished, as we sat around waiting for the racing to begin. All types of track people sat in, and for the most part these were people knew horses and not much else. One of my good friends was a veterinarian, Dr. Pete Hall, and he was a Racetrack Rummy regular. Any time one of my guys would be running a horse, I would pass it by Pete and he might tell me, "'Watch it, that horse has a bad ankle or maybe foot problems." I'd pass this info on to my jockey, but it sometimes also influenced whether or not I wanted to wager. I learned that the smallest tidbit you picked up from talking to a vet might turn out to be very useful information when passed on to the jockey. The more the jockey knew about the horse, the better he could ride it.

Dr. Peter Hall, a leading veterinarian, grew up on horse farms; his father Norm Hall was champion professional jumping rider. The senior Hall's first job was on a horse farm in Medford, MA right after Pearl Harbor when Pete, one of five children, was five-years old. Pete and Joe would become lifelong friends and he remembers Joe's early days at Garden State:

"I don't remember how he got started, but Joe began working as a jockey agent. He was always pumping me for information and we became very close friends. His was a face that first became familiar because he was always hanging around the track. At the noon hour every day we used to get a card game called Racetrack Rummy going in a rec hall off the backstretch of the track. We usually had three or four games going on, consisting of four people playing four hands. The games ranged from ten cents a point to a dollar. At first Joe would watch the games, then one day he jumped in and he loved it.

"We were all horse people, and during the game Joe might ask, "Who do you like; who do you like?' or '"Who are you taking care of?' I might tell him, 'I think this horse is nice', and I helped him make a few bucks. He was never a big gambler, maybe 10 or 20 dollars. I wouldn't have messed with him if he was playing any-thing bigger.

"That's how I got to know Joe and how he got to know a lot of other horse peo-ple. He was a very likable guy, he loved being around us and he was a smart guy who was becoming very knowledgeable listening to us gab about horses.

"I eventually moved to Miami for the winter and also started spending more time at Keeneland in Kentucky. They had all types of auctions there and I was brought on to look at and evaluate the horses. Then I was the one who hired other vets to do the same thing. I eventually started spending more time in the south and less in New Jersey as many of the trainers began seeing less need to send their horses

north.

> *"Racing in New Jersey was starting to come to an end as we knew it around the time Atlantic City opened for business. We used to have the race meet circuit that went from Garden State to Monmouth, Atlantic City, then back to Garden State October 1. Racing at Delaware Park and in Maryland became more popular and people stopped going to Atlantic City and Monmouth."*

Pete Hall also saved me load of money when I was in the casino business. Someone had given me a tip to buy stock in the company owned by Bob Brennan when he was rebuilding Garden State Racetrack. I bought about $10,000 worth of stock and happened to be talking to Pete that night. I paid about $10 a share and Pete told me to sell that stock immediately. I was up all night, nervous as could be, and first thing the next morning sold everything and got most of my money back. The following day the stock went down to something like ten or twenty cents a share.

One of the trainers I became friendly with, W.R. 'Billy' Prickett, pointed me in the direction of someone who would become my most successful rider. W.R. probably had about 50 or 60 horses and he had a young guy, John "Jake" Nied Jr., who was probably about 24 or 25 at the time. He had been hanging around the barn since he was a teenager, taking the horses out for gallops and doing other odd jobs. You have to understand that most apprentices start riding when they are about 16 or 17. Jake hadn't had that actual apprentice riding experience, but Billy pegged him as someone who had potential and advised me to sign him to a jockey contract. Billy said that he had enough confidence in this kid that he was going to have him ride everything in his barn and that I would be smart to get in early with Jake. I went to a big-time attorney in Camden, John Asbell, and had him draw up a contract that would bind Jake and me together for a year.

> *John "Jake" Nied is a member of the Pennsylvania Thoroughbred Horsemen's Hall of Fame and was one of the first jockeys to sign on with fledgling agent Joe Pagliei. They would enjoy a successful run together. He recalls his years with Joe:*
> *"I had been hanging around racetracks, mostly Monmouth Park, for about 9-½ years when Billy Prickett asked me to ride for him. It was during the last two weeks of the 1974 season and Billy had some extra horses that he wanted me to get on. I had other opportunities in the past, but they were mostly small outfits with maybe 8-10 horses. I wanted something better and damn I was prepared to wait for the right opportunity. Over the past 10 or 11 years Billy had established himself as one of the leading trainers in the game and he had about 60 or 70 horses. He liked the way I rode and asked if I would ride for his outfit. So here I am, young, married and off to Garden State with the best trainer in the business, who would also become a very close friend. Billy told me that I should get an agent. He didn't like many agents, but he did like Joe Pagliei and advised me to sign with him.*
> *"Joe was a nice guy with a good personality who got along with everybody. There were other agents who were nice guys, but I think what separated Joe was that he was a professional athlete who also played football at a big-time college. He understood athletes and he loved sports. He just had to stay in sports and be*

around athletes. Joe and I also got along because we both loved horses and being around the track, but neither of us was born into it. Most people think that I came from a racing family because my younger brothers also became jockeys, but I'm the one who started it all. My grandfather had a produce farm in Egg Harbor. From the time I was seven until he died when I was 14, I spent every summer with my grandfather. Every morning he used to bring carrots and celery and other produce to the racetrack in Atlantic City and I would ride along with him. I fell in love in with horse racing just being around the jockeys and watching all the early morning racetrack activity. From that first summer of going to the track, I prayed every morning that I would become a jockey. Joe came to love the track the same way; it wasn't born into him."

Nied was happy to sign with me as an apprentice jockey. His fifth race in the book, he rode a winner for Prickett. This was unheard of as it was rare for an apprentice to even get into a race during their first year, let alone win one. Within about six months, Jake was one of the most highly-regarded jockeys in the area. He had the touch, he got on a horse and it would run. Almost immediately I was getting calls from all over, "I want that kid Jake on my horse." Jockeys were classified as an apprentice during their first year of racing, meaning that they had a five-pound allowance each race. Any horse that had a non-apprentice rider during that year had to carry an extra five pounds of weight.

He also set himself apart in other ways. Unlike most jockeys, he was well-spoken, very neat and always showed up on time. He was also extremely observant of his mounts. He would ride for the trainers in the morning and as soon as he got off a horse he would offer his evaluation with a statement like, "You can't run him, he has a bad foot; or bleeds from the mouth; or has sore throat; or you can't touch his back because it's tender." The trainers used to say, "Christ, that kid knows more about the horse than my grooms." Jake stayed with me the whole time I was in the business. Jake was the one jockey that I had an exclusive contract with. Billy Prickett warned me that once this kid started racing, everyone was going to try and get him to ride for them. Billy was right. Today, Jake is enshrined as member of the Pennsylvania Thoroughbred Horsemen's Hall of Fame, which is located at Parx Racing.

Rita Pagliei also remembers as Jake as being neatly dressed, but he also had a unique clothes shopping secret:
"Jake was always dressed well, but he hated shopping. His wife was about the same size as him and she used to go shopping in the boys, or even sometimes the girls, section of clothing stores. She would try a pair of pants on first and if they fit her, she would buy them for Jake."

Jake was winning, I was developing a good reputation around the track, and all these other jockeys came looking for me. A lot of the jockeys were cocky and they would walk around telling agents, "You should come with me, I got the business." When they came to me, I'd turn around and tell them, "I'VE got the business." I was getting to know the trainers and owners and the riders came to realize that I could get them good horses. As an agent you could only represent two riders at a given time, either one veteran and one apprentice, or two veterans. I took care of the big-time owners and if they had an important race coming up, they would call me and tell me that they wanted to put my kid on their horse. There were always about 20 or 25 other agents buzzing around the track, but as my reputation grew, I didn't have to get caught up in any competitive recruiting situations, people were coming to me first. I had both the jockeys and trainers calling me. This was a word of mouth business. Because Jake Nied was a very gifted rider, he was also always getting calls directly and he would simply tell them to call his agent.

Jake began getting calls to race in New York. The clerks of scale were strict up there and Jake and I learned to deal with traffic getting to the tracks. All jockeys had to be onsite and dressed in their silks two hours before a race. There were times we would be running late because of the New York traffic and I would have to jump out of the car, find a phone and let them know that we were on our way and only a few minutes away.

We used to get what was called a 'condition book' that we had to carry around the track. You would get a book three weeks before every race and I'd go around, meet with the trainers and open my book. A race would be three weeks out and I'd tell them I wanted to put my kid on their horse in this particular race or they might tell me that they wanted my kid for that race. If we agreed, I make that entry in the condition book.

My jockeys were always smart riders. They knew not to put a horse on the lead if the horse didn't run that way. There are three ways a horse can run, there's 'early speed,' 'middle speed' or 'come from the back.' The jockey has to know which category their horse falls into. You have to know how to let a horse run the way it likes to run. For instance, you don't hold an early speed horse back and save him for the stretch, you put him on the lead and let him run. If you try to make a horse run against his instincts, you won't get anything out of him. You also need to study what type of track a horse runs best on. For example, Atlantic City was a sandy track. We had horses that ran well at Garden State but couldn't get traction and handle the change in surfaces at Atlantic City. The hoof gets into the top surface and just doesn't go anywhere.

Gomer Evan was an Atlantic City trainer who was originally from Oklahoma. He went crazy when he found out that I was good friends with Tommy McDonald, who had been an All-American running back for the Sooners. Gomer asked me one day where 'Mon-Mooth' was. Someone suggested that he run one of his horses at Monmouth Park Racetrack, but he had never heard of it. He needed a rider for this particular horse, which happened to have massive hoofs. I supplied him with a jockey for the race in 'Mon-Mooth' and he was able to sneak the horse into a race and ended up winning, with the horse paying something like $100. He came back to Atlantic City with pockets full of cash, but had to give all the money back when it was learned that he had given the horse the wrong medication that day and it was running on something that shouldn't have been in its system. Gomer didn't care, he was happy that his horse had won.

Horses are very stubborn; they all have their own way of running. Jake Nied was wonderful at gauging a horse. He was always prepared, knew everything about his horses and how to make them winners. He could get on a mount that was never ridden before, take it around the track for a couple of weeks and he might say something like, "This horse can really run; he's fast coming out of the gate." Jake had a stutter when he was angry and if he ran a horse that lost, but had the ability to do better, he would jump off the horse and scream, "P-p-p-put me back on that damn horse, I know what he did wrong and I can win with him." I would write notes in the condition book with all of Jake's comments. I would get to him as soon as the race ended so I could get all of Jake's thoughts while they were still fresh in his head. If Jake said, "Get me back on that horse," I would immediately start looking for a claiming race for the horse. I'd look for, say a $10,000 race, and go up to the trainer and tell him that Jake really wants to ride his horse in this race. The trainer would say, "Let me look for a race," and I'd tell him that I already had it marked. The trainer might say, 'Well, if you really think he can win, let's hold him back and enter a $15,000 race." Jake could ride a horse once and know its value and how much it should run for.

Adele Paxson was a very successful horse breeder based in Bucks County. I had a rider from Texas, Mike Marley, who had a bad left shoulder and little use of his left arm. He'd never fully recovered from a broken shoulder and couldn't do anything with his left arm, but kept sticking his horses with his right hand. I told him to never tell anyone in the world that he couldn't stick with his left, because if other trainers or jockeys found out that he could only push to the left, they would run from that side. One time at Garden State, Mike rode a horse for Mrs. Paxson that he kept smacking on the head with his right hand, pushing the horse further and further to the outside. Mike must have figured that this horse couldn't run from the back, so he kept pushing it until came out of, and around, the pack. The horse was right up against the rail coming down the backside, pulled ahead and won. That night Mrs. Paxson called me at home and said that she wanted Mike Marley to ride all of her horses. She asked how much we wanted for 'first call,' meaning that we always had to be available to ride one of her horses. I didn't know how the hell to answer, so I just said, "How about $1,000 a month." She agreed, and when I told Mike Marley that we were getting a thousand a month, all he said was, "Wow." That went for me, too, as I was getting $250 of that. The Paxons had all top-bred horses and we won just about every two-year old race around. We weren't afraid to go anywhere: New York, Maryland; because we knew we always had the best horse on the track. In Atlantic City these horses just won going away with Mike riding them. Mike and I won a lot of races and made good money riding for Mrs. Paxson.

Billy Prickett had a horse, Al Battah, and he said to me, "Joe, this horse can really run. You can name your rider, but if you put Jake Nied on him, this horse will win every time." The horse won about four or five times in a row, but we raced him sparingly because Jake picked up that he had a bad knee. Because of Jake's observation, we learned to take our time with the horse. We'd give Al Battah a month or so rest between races, as opposed to running him every three weeks, in order to give him time for his knee to heal.

Once, we were scheduled to race one of Billy Prickett's horses in North Jersey and it was cold and snowing like hell. Billy told us to stop by his barn in Mt. Holly on the way up and he would explain to Jake the best way to ride the horse. We were running in a big race at the Meadowlands with a $50,000 purse. Billy wasn't going to make the trip and, as we stood in the barn, he was giving all these riding tips to Jake, who was a real cocky kid. Jake was nodding his head and agreeing with everything Billy said, "Yeah, yeah, yeah; good idea. I'll do that." We get in the car and Jake turns to me and says, "You know what Prickett told me to do: take this horse back to last, he has one good run in him. Break him slow and finish hard. That son-of-a-bitch is full of shit; he doesn't know anything about this horse. I'm gonna get on the lead right out of the gate and run him so hard that his ass is going to look like this," and he made a wide circle with his hands. "And when we finish the race his ass is still going to look that big," he said, as he made a tiny circle with his thumb and forefinger. Jake won the race by about 12 or 15 lengths. He was a smart kid. I listened to him as we drove through the snow to the Meadlowands, and he kept telling me, "Trust me Joe. I'm gonna put him on the lead and we're going to win."

We were a good team. It was a two-man deal, we were both always looking for horses that we could win on. If Jake was running against another horse that bumped him around, he'd finish the race and say to me, "Joe, get me on that other horse, the one that kept bumping me. I can win with him." I'd go to the trainer and tell him that his horse gets in a lot of trouble and I have a guy that can make him a winner. I'd open my book and look for a race three weeks out, put the horse in with my jockey and have the trainers sign the book. Jake would look for horses that got in trouble and say, "Joe, trust me. I can ride him the right way." In the interim before the next race, Jake would take the horse around the track and let him gallop around when there was no action. He'd let the horse run from the rail out. If he liked the horse, he would give the ok, this horse is sound, I'll ride him. He'd also give advice to the trainer, like this horse needs a tongue tie or a shadow rule. I'd also pump the vets for as much info as I could get, so between Jake and myself, we usually knew everything about a horse going into a race. I used to go around telling all of the trainers, "There's a need for Nied," adding that if they put Jake on their horse in say, the fifth race, they would win.

I'd also look at what was call 'the overnight,' those races that were scheduled in the next 48 hours and didn't have a jockey. I'd look for a horse that I knew had a history of bumping and put one of my guys on who I knew could ride it right.

As an agent, I got 25% of the jockey's winnings. Some of the jocks didn't want to pay up. In that case, I'd go to the racing secretary so that I knew exactly how much my jockeys had won the past week. Jake was never a problem, in fact sometimes he would slip me extra few bucks for spending time walking around the barn and talking to the trainers, or maybe buying a trainer or owner a drink or two. Carlos Lopez was one jock I always had to hound. He'd give me, "Oh, man, I don't have anything; I had a tough week." I'd tell him, "Bullshit, I know exactly how much you won. Give me my money." But we got along well, we understood each other. He knew I wasn't going to take any crap from him.

I met Carlos when he tapped me on the shoulder, introduced himself and proceeded to tell me that we could make a lot of money working together. I told him that was fine, as long as I got my 25% from the previous week every Monday. I also reminded him that we split, 50-50, any money either of us won on bets that were placed for us in races that he ran in. He agreed, "Okay boss; that's fine." First week we're working together he wins a race, and I have the binoculars on him as he brings the horse to the paddock area. I see the owner hand him a green $50 winner ticket and Carlos sticks it in his boot. The horse paid $20, so the ticket is worth $1000. I crossed the track and was waiting for Carlos at the bottom of the steps to the jockey room. He greets me, "Hey boss, we just had a nice day, $1200. Not bad." My cut would be $300. I said, "Yeah, that was great, but let me have the ticket." He's giving me the, "What ticket" business and I said, "Bullshit, give me the ticket." He tells me "Boss, you have eyes all over the place," as he pulls the ticket from his boot. I didn't want him cashing the ticket because I might never see my cut. I took the ticket to the window and cashed it. Carlos and I always made money together, but he kept me on my toes trying to collect it.

> *The track was full of Runyonesque characters, especially the jockeys. Carlos Lopez was a favorite of Rita Pagliei:*
> *"They were all characters; some of them were REAL characters, especially Carlos Lopez. I once asked him how many kids he had and he answers 'Oh Mrs. (he always called me 'Mrs.'), I haven't seen them in a long time, but thirteen that I know of'.*
> *"A funny story, one day when Joe was handling Carlos' book he stopped by our house. He was married to a woman named Millicent; she was very pretty, very sweet and had a very fair complexion. They had a couple of kids together and Millicent was a real homebody. Carlos' car was facing our house and he had a big, dark woman sitting inside. I told him to bring her inside, don't make her wait in the car. He says 'No, no Mrs.; she stays there, I have problem; one thing, she had baby. But it was a mistake and now Millicent wants to divorce me. I told him that I didn't blame her. He says 'But I named the baby Millicent Jr.' I swear to God, can you believe it; he thought he could appease his wife by naming the baby after her. He told her, 'But, I named the baby after you, Mommy'. No jury would have convicted her if she killed him on the spot.*
> *"Another time, Carlos came to our house, opens the trunk of his car and reaches into a locker that he had back there. The locker is full of cash and he starts counting out bills, hundreds and twenties. He hands me a wad of cash and says 'Please Mrs., please put this in the bank for me, it's very important'. I said. 'Maybe I will; maybe I won't, how do you know you can trust me?' He says, 'I trust you; I trust you... just get it in the bank, please'."*

The jockey I probably made the most money with was Bobby Colton. I averaged about $2,000 a week when we were working together. He was a funny guy. He never trusted anybody. When he first asked me to take his book, he said he wanted to work with me, but needed to wait a couple of weeks. I said to him, "What the hell do you want to wait for. I can put you on a bunch of winners right now." He answered that some of the other jockeys told him that I was too green, that I hadn't been around the track long enough. I told him that while I may not have been around as long as some of the other agents, I knew all of the owners and trainers and they were calling me. I had plenty of business and I told Bobby that if he had doubts that he should just go off and do what he wanted with someone else. He came back to me and said, "Let's do it. Take my book." The first afternoon he raced with me, I put him on five winners. I was putting him on horses that were winning by five or six lengths. He just had to guide them around the track.

An owner from Canada called and told me that he was entering a horse in a $200,000 race at Garden State and wanted me to ride it for him. I gave the race to Bobby Colton; the horse gets sent down and Bobby walks it around the track. He comes right over and says to me, "What are you, nuts; this horse is lame, he won't make it out of the gate." I'm concerned and I call the owner, who was a friend of mine, up in Canada and explain to him what Bobby had said. He tells me, "Don't worry about it; that's just the way the horse walks… trust me he's going to win." The horse goes off at 8-1 and Bobby brings him home a winner. He proceeds to tell me that he shouldn't have doubted me and that I know what I'm doing. I told him I'm not that smart, I just took the word of my friend. One thing I learned was that when you got a tip from an owner, it was usually good. The owner gets his information from the trainer, and while the trainer might bullshit other people, he's going to tell the owner the truth if he wants to keep his job. If the trainer tells the owner, "Go get a good rider for the next race, this horse can win," it's usually reliable information.

It also helped when a horse had a smart trainer and Charlie Robbins was one of the best. One guy came to him with a horse he picked up for about $7500. Charlie recognized that the horse had a hole it its foot, so he had a special shoe made up. The horse turned out to be a big winner and the owner did very well on the selling end.

Charlie was also the trainer I went to when I got a call from a friend at the Latin Casino informing me that Jack Klugman was in town for a performance there. Klugman loved the horses and was looking to spend some time at Garden State Racetrack which was located right across the road, Route 70, from the nightclub. The Latin Casino was one of the classiest dinner clubs on the East Coast; it seated about 2,000 with a Vegas-style dinner theater and was known as South Jersey's 'Showcase of the Stars.' It attracted the same level of entertainment as the Copacabana in New York. It lost most of its luster when Atlantic City opened and the casinos became sexier venues for high-end entertainment.

I went around the track telling people that I was bringing Jack Klugman over for the day and was looking for a good horse for him to bet. Charlie Robbins gave me a horse that he knew could win and would pay about $20.

I picked Jack up at the Latin and told him that I had one really good horse for him. Jack said that if he placed a bet the horse was sure to lose. We're sitting in our box as the horses come to the gate and I'm watching the odds drop on our horse. The horse comes from the back, wins, but only pays $12. Nevertheless, Jack was thrilled just to have a winner. He folded up his money, stuffed it in his pocket and I drove him back to the club. I get back to the track and run into Al Besselink, a professional golfer, all-around gambler and well-known ladies' man. I had given Al the same horse that I had given to Jack. I went up to Al and asked him how much money he placed on the race. He answered "Only $500," because that was all he had. I called him a son-of-bitch and told him that it was his late bet that drove the odds down. I also had money on the race. Jack Klugman was happy, Al Besselink was happy, but I wasn't too happy because Al's bet had cost me a few bucks.

Pattie Pagliei recalls the color and characters associated with the racetrack with great fondness:

"There were so many characters, and dad knew every one of them, or so it seemed. He would bring us to visit the jockeys and I was in love with the colors and the silks that they wore. That might be part of what influenced me to get into design and fashion. I was also in awe of the sports heroes and artifacts that he used to bring home with him. I remember him bringing home a pair of Wilt Chamberlain's sneakers; they were HUGE. I thought dad really does hang around with the big guys."

I'd say that it took me about two months to develop a good feel for the job. What I learned quickly was to get to know the trainers. I always made a point of wandering around shed row and talking with them. I'd keep a list of the top ten trainers, those who won the most races, and I would pick a specific horse with them and say, "Put me on that goddamn horse." I'd get them to open their book and commit to something like 'Next Thursday you'll ride this horse for me in the fifth race.' You had to consistently work the barn to get good mounts. I'd go up to them, name specific horses, point out their upcoming races and tell them they should put my guy on. They might say something like, "How the hell did you know about that race?" I'd show them my book and how it broke down all of the maiden races, maiden filly races, colt races, every possible race. The trainer might say I'm looking for a $15,000 race and I'd open my book, show him when the next one was coming up and tell him to put my kid on his horse. All the other jockey agents were always wondering how I did it and I never shared anything. I kept track of every horse, every race, especially looking for horses that I saw could run, but didn't know how to win. If I saw a horse that lost by five lengths, but looked good, maybe got bumped around too much, I'd go the trainer and tell him, "My jockey is smart, he'll know how to ride that horse. Put him on and he'll get it done."

I'd watch not only the live race, but also study the taped replay. I'd look for horses that got into trouble because of their jockey and I'd go that trainer and tell him that I have guy who will know how to ride that horse. I'd tell him that my guys don't make excuses, "Oh, I got bumped." My guys were smart and knew how to avoid trouble. I'd look for good horses that had the wrong rider. At the same time I was always on the lookout for smart jockeys who knew how to ride. After a couple of months I had jockeys coming up, tapping me on the shoulder and asking me to find them rides. They knew that I knew most of the big-time trainers and owners and if they wanted to ride the best, they should come with me.

I knew what kind of horse to match up with a jockey. Carlos Lopez was a front runner who loved to get out on the lead with a horse. He'd jump in front early, rest the horse a little on the backside, then, when he got to the head of the stretch he'd open it up again. If another horse was coming up along the outside he'd maybe give it bump and push it out further.

I learned from the smart jockeys to ride in the indented tracks left behind by tractors that pulled the gate to loosen the ground. The tire tracks pressed the ground in a bit and that was the hardest part of the track. I used to tell my jocks to follow the tractor tires and you can save yourself a little bit of work. I'd also tell my guys, that if they couldn't get in the lead early, they should start edging out to the rail so that they didn't have to make up too much ground trying to get outside at the end of the race.

I had also gotten to know all of the people in the office. Everybody carried a condition book. If a guy had a book, say for a Pennsylvania-bred horse that was running in Maryland, he would call me to help figure out where that horse best fit. I knew most of the horses, and I tell him, "I'll put this jockey on that horse." I'd get out to the track about 5:45 the next morning and take the jockey over to meet the horse. We'd spend time with the trainer, and my guy would take the horse out for a little bit. The jockey would come back and depending on how the ride went he might say, "This horse is shit," or "This horse can really run."

At first the jockeys didn't think I knew what I was talking about, but as they saw how hard I worked, they'd say, "Hey man, you're always around. You're always talking to the right people, maybe you do know something."

Back to that wannabe jockey I mentioned on page 45. Some guys just didn't have it when it came to being a jockey. If I had been more successful turning this guy into a decent rider, the streets of Philadelphia might have been a lot calmer and the headlines of the Philadelphia Daily News less colorful in the 1980's and early '90:

A guy called and told me that a bug rider was looking for an agent. I was always looking for another jock, so I agreed to take him. A skinny Italian kid from South Philly shows up, his name was Joey Merlino. He was about the right size and weight and I took him over to the stables. Every horse goes out on the track every day for exercise. Later in the morning I go back to that barn and the trainer tells me to get that kid out of here, he got thrown on his ass by the horse. I decide to give him another chance and the next day Joey comes back and I bring him to another barn. Same result. At that point I tell the kid that there is no point in coming back, the only talent he seemed to have was falling off horses. At that time nobody knew who he was or who he would turn out to be. Little did I know what the future would hold in store for Joey Merlino. He had no talent when it came to horses, but he did make a name for himself as the Boss of the Philadelphia Mob. I might have changed the course of Philadelphia crime lore if I could have made a jockey out of Skinny Joey Merlino.

One well-regarded horseman I became good friends with was Bob Levy, owner of Robert P. Levy Stables, a very successful racing and breeding operation. One of Bob's horses, Bet Twice, won the Belmont Stakes in 1987, and he also had a couple of horses that won the Eclipse Award as the nation's outstanding sprint horse. Bob would make sure that his trainer, Jimmy Croll, always saved a few horses for me. I'd run into Bob at the track and he'd say, "I'm going to put you on a winner."

George Cusimano, a jockey from Maryland came up to see me. He tapped me on the shoulder and said that he had heard positive things and wanted me to take his book. He said that I had a reputation as a good agent and that he had a lot of business and needed someone to handle it for him, and boy did he have a lot of business. After about a week we were doing really well, he knew all of the trainers and they were all trying to put him on a horse. He needed me to set his book for him. I got a call from a guy in Canada and he wanted me to put Georgie on a horse that was going to race in two days. I put Georgie on the horse and, when the overnights came out, I showed him the book. Georgie took a look at and said, "You have me on that horse from Canada, I can't ride it, that owner owes me money." I told him not to worry about it, that horse was going to win and he'd get his money that way. Georgie said that might be the best horse in the race, but he wasn't going to win if he didn't ride him. I said, "Come on, this is a guaranteed winner." He couldn't get over the fact that the owner never paid him from the last race and on that principle he passed on a sure winner.

I had a good run at Garden State. If that track hadn't of burned down, I'd be sitting on a lot of money today. It was the 1970's and I was bringing home at least $2200 a week. I walked around that track and had earned the confidence of everyone that mattered including the owners, trainers and jockeys. I was set up pretty well, not to mention that it was a good life hanging around the racetrack all day. The only bad part of the job was having people hit me up for tips and after awhile, whenever anybody asked me who I liked in particular race, I'd answer "Nobody." If you gave a guy a winner, he would always be up your ass begging for another one. If your horse lost, all I'd hear is, "You don't know what the hell you're talking about." "I don't like anybody today," became my stock answer. I learned that lesson from smart trainers like Gordon Potter, Glen Hill and Bobby Camac. If you give a guy a winner, he's the first person you're going to see the next day, hitting you with the same question, "Who do you like today." I also resented the fact that people were trying profit off of my hard work. When you wake up at five every morning, spend five or six hours at the track, go home and have lunch, then spend another three or four hours at the track, you don't want to give information away.

I did have a couple of priests that always I tried to take care of. If I liked a horse or two, I'd give the tip to them, always reminding them not to tell anybody else. I figured I could trust two priests to remain silent. They'd go off and bet their 10 or 20 dollars and from what I recall, they always did pretty well. I always tried to take care of the clergy. We used to race at night under the lights in Atlantic City. Rita and I had bought a house outside Atlantic City and Bobby Colton, one of my really good riders, came down to race. He rode a winner for me and the next morning I get a knock on my front door, it's Msgr. Clark from the local church in Northfield. Being a Catholic, I went to church regularly and he knew me from there. We made some small talk, then he asked me if liked any horses running that night and I gave him a winner. The next Sunday I'm standing on the communion line at the far left side of the church. Msgr. Clark was giving out the communion hosts on the other side of the church and when he saw me he came over and personally gave me my host. He liked going to the track with a couple of other priests and, whenever I could, I gave them a horse that I liked.

A smart hustler named John Kennedy had his own clientele and he'd go over and whisper to one of his guys, "I like this horse in the fifth race, put down $20 for me," because he didn't want anyone else to know who he liked. He was afraid that if people saw him at the betting window, they'd rush over and bet the same horse he did and cause the odds to drop. He knew horses and could watch a race better than anyone I ever knew. He could pick up if a jockey was pulling a horse and that's what got him in trouble. He would ask me, "Joe, did you learn anything looking at the racing form today?" He would look at that day's form with me, point at a horse and be able to explain exactly why that horse got in trouble or didn't run well last time out. The notes might say that horse went five wide to the outside, and John would say, "Bullshit, that horse got pushed eight wide to the fence." He always had the best information. Not many people liked him because he was kind of smug and abrasive, but I always got along with him. He loved to talk football and he'd build me up like I was Chuck Bednarik or some other legend whenever he introduced me. When I was with John I was always explaining to people that I was no star.

I used to get to the track at 5 am every morning. At 5:30 I'd head into the lunch room for a cup of coffee and everybody would be there: trainers, jocks, grooms, other agents. I'd get caught up with what was going on that day and I might have a trainer call me over with, "Hey Joe, can you get me a rider for so-and-so." All these little jockeys would come up and say, "Joe, I want you to take my book," and I'd tell them I had to watch them ride first. I got the reputation for not only being smart, but picking the right jockeys. I might see a guy on the track and, if I liked the way he rode, I would give him card and tell him to call me, I could get him a lot of good rides. In many cases I'd get a call a few months down the road. I also had to be convinced that the rider could maintain his weight. They had to be able to pack 112, 113 pounds. If they swelled up to say 121 pounds, that was too much. I also looked for jockeys who could talk intelligently to the owners and trainers. Most of these guys never finished high school, but they had to be able to explain to a trainer what was really going on with a horse.

Some trainers didn't really care to hear what a jockey had to say because they thought they knew it all, but the good ones usually listened and I wanted riders who understood their horses. The owners and trainers all had their own particular ways of doing things and it took a while to learn this, but after a while I figured out what it took individually to get through to them. You had to know what they did and didn't want to hear. Personally, I've never ridden a horse and was never around them growing up, but I was both smart and lucky enough to develop access to the right people. If I had to know something, I knew who to ask, and most of the guys I ran around with were pretty honest. If at 8 o'clock in the morning I had to make a change on that day's schedule, say if a horse came up lame or a jock was having a problem, I knew what call to make. I was always organized and had a plan ready for an emergency situation.

I became friendly enough with one owner that he got into the habit of naming horses after me, none of which performed very well. I was telling Joe DiMaggio about this and he advised me, "Joe, don't ever put your name on a horse unless you know he can run. Hold out for a real good horse." DiMaggio had plenty of experience, it seemed that almost every day someone was naming a horse after some variation of his name. I was always coming across horses named 'Joe D' or 'Yankee Clipper.' Unfortunately I never got a 'Joe Pag' horse that was any good.

A good friend of mine, John Servis was the trainer of Smarty Jones, the horse that won the Kentucky Derby and Preakness. I still run into John at the track. He always wants to talk football and I pump him for info on the horses that are running that day. John is one of the best people you'll ever find around the racetrack, a good solid person and a real family man.

Some of the trainers were either full of shit or simply didn't know what they were doing. Those guys, I wouldn't even bother to ask who they liked that day. You'd get a case where a guy's horse would win and you'd ask the trainer how much he put down on that race. You knew the guy bet on his horse, but he would come back at you with an answer like, "I had no idea he could win." It could also work the other way, say a trainer had a horse that was running lame. If he wanted to get back at a pain-in-the-ass bettor who kept bothering him, the trainer would give him the name of the lame horse and tell the guy to go out and bet on him just to get rid of him. They also learned like I did with Al Besselink, somebody might put a large last minute bet on a horse and drive the odds down. Another reason you learn to keep your mouth shut is that you know what simple eavesdrop can lead to. There was an instance when someone overheard a trainer telling me that he liked a particular claim horse in the fifth race, the guy who was listening in ran out and bought the horse. I was never a big bettor, but I'd bet on my guys, of course, when I felt good about a race. In some instances, I'd even bet against my guy. For example, if I knew one of my jocks was taking a horse out in a race just to give it run, I'd stay away. I never bet a lot, maybe $10-20 dollars on a horse. I made more money finding winners for my jockeys, so that's where most of my attention went.

Bobby Camac was another top trainer at Philadelphia Park and he was also involved with the breeding of Smarty Jones for Roy Chapman, the owner of Someday Farm. I used to meet him for an occasional dinner or lunch. He'd always grab the check, even if I was doing well at the time. Bobby would always say, "You're not making enough money to pay for this." If he liked any of the horses that were running that day he'd ask if I brought my 'betting money.' When Bobby told me that a horse was going to win, it would win. I had a female jockey named Rolanda Simpson and Bobby told me to put her on one of his horses in the eighth race at Delaware Park. The day of the race, I missed the exit when we were getting near the track and Rolanda got pretty nervous and upset. We made it inside just in time and her horse won, paying about 6-1; Rolanda was so happy.

Tragically, Bobby had some real problems to deal with in life. His second wife's son had a big-time drug problem and was always taking money from them, either grabbing cash or writing checks from their account. In 2001, Bobby got into a major argument with the kid and the next day he came over to their house and shot both Bobby and his wife dead. With Bobby gone, Chapman decided to sell most of his horses. A friend of Bobby's convinced him to hold on to Smarty Jones, and Smarty's success at the Derby and Preakness can be viewed as a tribute to Bobby Camac.

Dennis Heimer was another great trainer who knew everything about the horses he worked with. When he told you he liked a horse, you could take it to the bank. He used to give me, maybe, one or two horses a week. He would always add a personal guarantee, along the lines of, "If this horse doesn't win, the grandstand will collapse" or "This horse is so good, he can fall down at the gate and still win." He was known around the track as "Goose" because he was always stretching his neck to look at someone's Daily Racing Form. He won six training titles at Keystone and in 1982 ranked ninth in the entire nation with 130 wins. He was only 42-years old when he died of a heart attack in 1989. Like Bobby Camac, we lost him way too soon and I still miss both of them.

Today, my best source for tips is probably Kieron Magee. For my money he is the best trainer in Maryland and he knows ankles and knees like no one in the business. My son Joe is very tight with Kieron and lives in a house on his property in Maryland. I get together with Kieron when he comes up to Delaware Park Racetrack. His tips are very accurate, if Kieron Magee tells you that he likes a horse, listen closely and head to the betting window.

Another trainer, Joe Marquette, had a great horse named Gallant Bob. He could win races up to 7/8 mile. I put one of my older riders on Gallant Bob, the guy ran a terrible race and Gallant Bob came in second. After the race, Marquette pulled me aside and told me to never bring that jockey around the track again.

My favorite horseracing family has to be the Rooneys. Art Rooney, the founder of the Pittsburgh Steelers, was one of the all-time great gentlemen of sports. I think he took a special interest in me because of my football background. His twin sons, John and Pat, were in charge of Keystone and their father told them to take care of me. The twins were also terrific people and they pretty much gave me the run of the track.

I could not have been happier. There was no better environment than being around the Garden State racetrack every day. I was going to bed about 8, 8:30 every night and getting up before 5; I looked forward to every day. I lived just a few minutes away and was making very good money doing something I loved. Things could not have been better. I could not have been happier doing anything else, except maybe playing football. I talked to all the owners and trainers, met them for dinners and lunches, and invited them to the house for meals and watching races. These contacts would also come in handy later as many of them followed me to the casinos in Atlantic City after everything literally went up in flames for me on April 14, 1972.

It was a sunny Thursday afternoon and I was watching the race from the box seat section, maybe 30 feet from the Colonial Room Restaurant, located on the second floor. Somebody in the seats started shouting that there was smoke coming from the restaurant dining room. We went inside to look and flames were shooting out of one of the wall plug receptacles. I was one of the first in the room and, along with some others, started throwing water at the flames. It seemed the more water I threw, the higher the flames went. The flames were rising toward the ceiling as we tried to put out the fire. A few people were looking for fire extinguishers, but none could be found. At that point no one thought this was a serious fire.

I ran outside, facing Route 70, smoke was billowing all around and I saw some of the jockeys leaning out a window. The jockey room was located on the second floor above where I was standing. Jake Nied was one of the jocks at the window and I started yelling to him to get his ass out of there. He yelled back that he wasn't leaving until he got all of his equipment out first. He started throwing his boots, whip, tack and silks, all the tools of his trade. The fire department showed up and ran a ladder up to the window to get the jocks down. Jake climbed down, but not until he had thrown all his equipment out, which I gathered up for him.

From there the fire just erupted and went crazy. The grandstands were made of wood, except for the steel support beams, and it probably only took about 10 minutes for the fire to spread from one end of the stands to the other. Within about 25 minutes the entire track was on fire. There were over 10,000 people at the track that day, and by some miracle only three lives were lost: one employee, one patron and one firefighter.

I saw women, accompanied by security, carrying containers of cash out of the burning offices. At the back side, the horsemen from the stable area were trying to get the horses out to a safe area. Horses are stubborn and it's not easy to get them to do something they aren't accustomed to.

We just stood back and watched. Because the fire was being fueled mostly by wood, the firemen realized there wasn't much they could do other than containment. All around us people were crying, not knowing if a friend or family member or co-worker got out.

Rita has clear memories of that day:
"Jake was racing that day and Joe was yelling at him from the ground to jump from the window of the jockey room. Poor Jake, he weighed about 105, maybe 110 pounds at most, and Joe telling him to jump. It's amazing that so few people died. There was another person who was reported missing. I'm surprised that nothing was written or a movie made about that missing person. Joe said there were people running back and forth with baskets full of cash; I don't know, maybe that person disappeared with some of that cash."

Horse racing was still extremely popular in New Jersey. On any given day the parking lot and the stands would be packed. Garden State was a very successful racetrack with prestige races that attracted some of the best horses from around the county for big races like the Jersey Derby or Garden State Stakes. People would get dressed up for a day at the track: the guys in jackets and ties, the women in dresses and fancy hats. Garden State was part of the "Golden Triangle" of New Jersey Racing along with the Atlantic City Race Course and Monmouth Park Racetrack. We'd race 30-60 days at each track, moving from Garden State to Atlantic City to Monmouth, doing this circuit twice a year.

When Garden State burned down, we had to move all of the horses that were housed there to new homes. All of the horsemen were scrambling to find a track that had room for their horses. No one knew where to go; this was not a situation where you had a contingency plan in place. There were a lot of us that were doing well at Garden State: owners, trainers, grooms, jockeys, agents and all the rest.

Before the fire erupted, I figured I was set for the rest of my life.

Joe Pagliei Jr. vividly recalls the Garden State fire and its effect on his dad:
"The fire was devastating for him and our family. He had established himself there, had a couple of the top riders and was finally at the point where he was making good money. We lived about five minutes away from the track in Pennsauken and he had four kids. He had been scuffling to pay bills and had now reached a point where he was doing well and it was taken away by the fire. It set us back a bit.

"He was now running around to try and make a buck. It was really tough on dad. He'd go down to Atlantic City or Maryland and stay overnight to try and

61

make a living.”

Patti Pagliei recalls some dark moments but also recalls the great resolve of her parents following the fire:

"When Garden State Racetrack burned down, mom and dad struggled to get by. I don't know how they managed with four kids and dad being out of work, but somehow we got through it. We survived on hotdogs instead of hamburgers; pasta and simple foods and going to church to pray for the next job to come along."

Rita recalls the fire:

"My mother, living in West Philly, knew about the fire before me. From her window she saw smoke coming from New Jersey and called to ask me if the racetrack was on fire. This was before the days of cell phones and I couldn't get hold of Joe. I turned on the KYW (Philadelphia's all-new radio station) and after a while finally heard about the fire. Joe comes with Jake, who was wearing one boot, his pants and no shirt. He looked like someone who had just escaped from a fire. I told him call his wife and let her know he was alright. Joe was thinking, 'Oh shit; I'm making more money than I ever made and the track burns down'. He had the leading jockeys and they were making a lot of money. But it was a tough life, especially in the winter; the track was only open so many days."

Jake Nied recalls the Garden State fire:

"The entire New Jersey horse racing scene was hurt by the Garden State fire. By the time the track was rebuilt, people who had supported it in the past and came every day just didn't seem to think that there was a need for it. The project was delayed because the Mayor of Cherry Hill at the time (Maria Greenwald) didn't want the track to come back. Cherry Hill was building up and she was concerned about traffic during the day and thought the property could be put to a better use. When the racetrack was rebuilt, one of the conditions was that there was no more day racing during the week and people who had been used to coming to the track in the afternoon just didn't respond to night racing. The old timers, the guys who used to carry the Racing Form with them everywhere, disappeared. They were never replaced by a new pack of younger guys who lived by the Racing Form. It hadn't been that long of a gap between the old and the new track, but the old days didn't come back.

"There were other outside factors that coincided. I remember a guy telling me that phone betting was just around the corner. I never saw that coming, you couldn't find any pay phones around a racetrack because they didn't want guys calling their bookies when there was a last minute change in a race. But phone betting came in and you could dial in from anywhere and make a bet. Then simulcasting became popular and you could watch a race without coming to the track. With phone betting and simulcasting, there was no need to show up. On top of that, it was Atlantic City that delivered the final blow in killing racing in New Jersey as people were now taking their fun money down there.

"Everything was factored against Garden State. Winter racing was taking off.

Horses and jockeys used to come up here after the Florida season, but now the horses didn't bother since the owners and trainers had found new homes.

"Billy Prickett took all 50 or 60 of his horses to Maryland and Joe and I went with him. We'd stay down there for a couple of days at time, commuting back and forth to New Jersey. We'd rode Billy's horses and it turned out that they just didn't fit down there. We probably ran about 100 races and we couldn't win anything. The Maryland-bred horses were just a tad better. We might put a horse that we had success with in New Jersey in a $20,000 Claimer race in Maryland. Our horses never won, they were always a grade behind. We would have to enter our $20,000 New Jersey horse in a $15,000 race in Maryland. A $20,000 Claiming Race in New Jersey simply wasn't as good as the same race in Maryland. They just had a better grade of horses; I'd say at least 20-30% better than the New Jersey horses. And there were a lot more of them. The field was deep in most races and nearly all of them could run.

"We didn't do well in Maryland. It was tough to get stall space. They might tell us that we could race at a particular track, but there was no room to keep the horse there. They'd send us to some farm miles away and just have us ship the horses in when it was time to run. Joe and I tried commuting back and forth to New Jersey, but between travel expenses, lodging, meals, we weren't making any money. It was a closed, clubby operation. They took care of the locals. No matter how good a rider you had, and I was one of the best, you couldn't win if you couldn't get on a good horse. It was a tough scene to break into. They'd tell us, 'Yeah, yeah; we're gonna get you a ride', but they would end up sloughing us off and giving the best horses to the guys that they knew.

"Joe was good enough as an agent that he could have re-established himself anywhere. This just goes to show what a good family man he is. He had four kids and a nice house right near the Betsy Ross Bridge. Going back and forth to Maryland was tough on him, as it was for me. He just decided that he needed to be in New Jersey and that's what I believe more than anything pushed him out of racing and into Atlantic City."

Jake could ride anywhere, but most of my connections were through Garden State. Even in terms of the New Jersey circuit, the Garden State horses were a notch below those that ran at Monmouth. Because they had better horses, Monmouth also attracted better jockeys. Many of the best jockeys went down to Florida to ride the good horses during the winter. These guys had their own representation and, if I took their book, I just didn't have the same connections at Monmouth. I had established myself at Garden State, basically by being there every day, and I would have to start all over at Monmouth.

My son Joey learned the business the right way in Maryland. He started on the ground floor and got to know the owners and trainers just like I did at Garden State. He became best friends with Kieran McGee, who is probably the leading trainer in Maryland. He got to know all the right people and became a successful jockey agent. Joey's now an executive with the Stronach Group, a company that owns and operates racetracks all over the country. They're also into simulcasting and off-track betting.

Joey followed my Garden State blueprint and it worked for him, but it was a little late in the day for me to start all over in a new market.

Bob Brennan, a securities investor, rebuilt Garden State and opened in 1985. It was gorgeous, as nice as any racetrack in the country. But it was too late, the track never came close to bringing back the glamour and excitement, by that time most of the horsemen had wandered off and were established at other tracks. Keystone Park, in Bensalem just outside of Philadelphia, had been purchased by ITB and was renamed Philadelphia Park. They were operating a top-quality racing program over there and, in the absence of Garden State, had established it as the pre-eminent track in the area. Atlantic City was by now about the hottest destination on the East Coast, and gamblers were flocking there. They ran the last race at Garden State in 2001, the property was torn down and now it's a shopping center.

By the time the new Garden State Racetrack had opened, I was getting established in Atlantic City.

Ex-Bird Roots for Namesake Horse

Pagliei's Pride and Joy Has Four Legs

for now he must settle for fulfilling the role of a favorite conversation piece on the Bell's backstretch.

Clark, 45, possesses a subtle sense of humor along with a knack for quickly making friends.

And a little more than a year back, his affinity for football and friendship with gabby, assistant Eagles coach Gummy Carr brought him into contact with Joe Pagliei of Pennsauken, N.J., pads and two legs.

AN INSTANT friendship was the end result. The two men went out a couple of times, had some laughs together and before Pagliei knew what hit him, Clark the defensive back, had named one of his young homebreds after the ex-Bird.

Joe Pagliei is so thrilled at the honor bestowed upon him by friend Clark that he visits his namesake at least a couple of times a week, even looks in on him on Sundays.

"I've never seen him run yet," said Pagliei, now an auto salesman. "But I'll be there when he wins. It doesn't matter whether it's at Liberty Bell, Atlantic City or Monmouth. I'll be there. I've gotten so enthused about this thing. It's like I own a part of him."

And when Pagliei does win, the champagne's on Jumpin' Joe.

"I'll do the buying, that's for sure," he said. "I feel as though I have to buy. My whole family is involved in this. They'll wait until he runs and wins."

Even Joe's father, a 66-year old retired steelworker in Pittsburgh, is a member of the horse Pagliei's small but select club.

WHEN MAX told me about the horse, I called my father and told him they named a horse after our name. He went right into Italian club in Pittsburgh and told all of his friends.

He was really proud and then one old guy in the back sat with a thick Italian accent, "But, Al, what will happen if they dope your horse? That won't be so good for your name."

Pagliei laughed and said his father shot right to the phone and called Joe with his worries. But the ex-gridder satisfied that they had no problems on this count and old Al is once again one hundred percent behind the young runner.

Clark, delighted with Pagliei's reception here, gets even with laughs about the whole thing when he kiddingly expressed the hope the young fellow can run faster than the old one he's named after.

Clark said Pagliei has run three times, getting and a third in maiden events.

He showed potential, but was an unruly sort, him gelded.

"I think he might be better now," he said. "He businesslike in his works and he's gained some w. he's improved physically and is stronger now. He playful the other way."

CLARK FEELS Pagliei will be ready to run i weeks.

Pagliei, unfortunately, does not rate as the cl stable. That honor has been accorded Street Pain defeated in a photo finish earlier this meet.

"That was his first time around two turns," sa of Street Painter. "He's a big, long-striding h seemed to have a little trouble handling the course

"He's a very unusual horse because he isn't horse around. He had major surgery, chips remo left knee, a year ago. He has some pain once in he'll run right up against it.

"I think he would have been a top horse if h injured. But it's sort of touch and go with him i hoping he stays together."

Clark's big hope for the future is no longer r was the speedball daughter of Lucky Debonair na Luck. She won her first two starts with chips in She finished second next out and is now waiting Fiddle Isle, the world record holder for 1½-miles.

7 – BALLYS

It's tough to imagine a more energized and exciting place than Atlantic City in the 1980's. I was fortunate enough to back into the casino business while it was still in its infancy. The novelty of the East Coast was accompanied by all kinds of excitement and, while I was interested in what was going on down there, I never would have made the move if not forced by circumstance. If Garden State Racetrack had not burned to the ground, I would have been more than happy to continue as a jockey agent. The racing business was doing well by me, in the 1970's I was bringing home about $2,000 a week.

I didn't know what I was going to do next. There were other tracks on the East Coast and I had experience and familiarity with most of them, but Garden State was my home track. It was in my backyard and all of my important industry connections were there. I had a wife and four children, a mortgage, no job and no immediate prospects for employment. Working as a journeyman jockey agent running up and down I-95 between New York and Maryland wasn't putting much food on my table. I decided to go down the shore and find out about all of the noise and fanfare that was coming out of these new casinos.

I took a ride down to Atlantic City and visited with two old friends, Matty Goukas and Jimmy Orr, who were both working at Caesars. Both had been professional athletes. Matty was a local guy who had gone to St. Joseph's and played for a bunch of NBA teams, including the 76ers. After leaving Atlantic City he would coach the Sixers and Orlando Magic. Jimmy played ball at three different colleges, one of which was Clemson and he and I had developed a Tigers' connection that remains today. He had his best professional years catching passes from Johnny Unitas with the Baltimore Colts. It was Jimmy who once told me that he got his big break when he was a rookie with the Pittsburgh Steelers and all of the guys listed ahead of him got hurt and created an opening for him to play. He added that it was too bad the guys in front of me on the depth chart always seemed to stay healthy. I was telling Matty and Jimmy that I was out of work and had a family to take care of, and they both told me, "Joe, with your connections to sports and the racetrack, you should work down here. You should get into this business; you'd be great." They encouraged me to apply to the casinos, especially Bally's, which was the place to see and be seen with professional athletes.

I put together a resume, sent it over to Bally's and got a phone call from Al Rosen inviting me for an interview. I was thrilled, but realized I had a bit of a clothing problem. I had spent most of the past decade or so working at racetracks and, while I always liked to look good, I wasn't wearing suits while hanging around the paddocks. I go through my closet and find that I don't have any job interview clothes, at least any that fit. I had an acquaintance, Mitch Daroff, whose family operated Daroff and Sons, a top-of-the-line men's shop at 23rd and Walnut. The Daroffs also manufactured the Botany 500 line of suits and sports coats. I called Mitch and explained my dilemma:

I needed to look good, money was tight and I didn't have the cash to pay for the clothes. Mitch told me not to worry about it, he was going to dress me up to guarantee that I got the job and I could pay him then. You might say that I had to take out a marker to buy my Atlantic City interview suit. When Mitch got through with me: suit, shirt, tie, shoes, the works, I never looked better. That day, when I walked into Mitch's shop, I didn't own a single suit, within a couple of years I could go two weeks without wearing the same suit. If I needed formal wear, I would go into the casino wardrobe department and one of their tailors would outfit me in a custom-fit tux. From there I was taking limos, helicopters and private planes to invitation-only events. Hell, my CEO would send a car and driver to pick me up for a racquetball game.

I left the interview with Al feeling pretty good about things, but still had some uncertainty, I didn't know anything about the casino business. Later I came to realize that with the lifetime skill set that I had developed this would turn out to be the best landing spot for me. Very few people going to work in Atlantic City in the 1970's and 80's had any casino experience, but I was equipped better than most to make a success out of it. In discussing my background these are some of the things that Rosen may have picked up on during our interview:

1   Clairton—I grew up around gambling. Hell, until I left for Clemson, I had spent my whole life living below Moe Martin's gambling parlor. I knew all the games, understood the language and terms and, maybe most important, understood gamblers and their psyche.

2   Professional Athlete—I looked and comfortably talked the part. I was a sports guy and this would prove to be of immense value, especially in establishing myself at Bally's where much of the marketing was built around having famous jocks hanging around the gamblers. Another bit of good fortune came from the fact that I had played in both Philadelphia and New York, the two markets that Bally's was looking to draw its customers from, especially high rollers. And, I was a competitor: it came naturally to me to outwork everybody else and do whatever it took to prepare to win.

3   Golf—The fact that I had a decent golf game would pay dividends for years, starting with my first week on the job. I carried an 18 handicap, but usually played better than that. So much of my casino entertaining would be done on the links.

4   Horse Racing—The overlaps between casinos and the racetrack are obvious. Everybody that sets foot in a casino or a racetrack does so with the expectation that this is going to be their day. At Garden State I was always surrounded by gamblers and many of them were prepared to follow me to Atlantic City for some action.

5   Me—I like to talk. I'm a people person and I've never been caught short for a story. A good trait to have when working with the public.

These are all things that come in handy as a casino host and made it easy for me to build relationships.

> *Joe Pagliei Jr. followed his father into the casino business, he remembers when his dad started working in Atlantic City:*
> *"It was tough on the family when Garden State burned down. Bally's was just the third casino to open in Atlantic City and dad got word that the old third baseman (Al Rosen) from the Cleveland Indians was hiring athletes to serve as hosts. Leonard Tose helped a lot and dad was hired with Bob Pellegrini and Oscar Robertson's brother Bailey. Dad was commuting from Pennsauken and one day he and my mom went down to the shore to look at houses. They found one they liked and came back and told us we were moving. I was a senior so it didn't affect me, but my two younger sisters were crying that they were moving away from their friends, but we moved to Northfield.*
> *"I was a big sports fan and we were meeting all of these athletes and entertainers and having them over to our house."*

I had no way of knowing it at the time, maybe Al Rosen and his boss Billy Weinberger saw it, but I was born and bred to be a casino host. If there were any doubts about hiring me, a chance meeting that I had shortly after the interview helped to seal the deal. Leonard Tose was a legend when it came to living big, he did everything to excess. Very few people got more out of life for their money that he did. Leonard even managed to get his money's worth when he was broke. He owned the Philadelphia Eagles and I was talking with him on the sideline during a visit to training camp. He asked how things were going and I told him that frankly, I wasn't doing well since the racetrack burned down. I mentioned my interview at Bally's and that I was waiting to hear back. He wished me luck and walked away. A few days later it would be Leonard Tose breaking the news to me that I had gotten the job. We were having dinner, the phone rings, Rita answers and voice on the other end tells her, "This is Leonard Tose, I'd like to speak with Joe." We thought he meant our son Joe Jr., who was working as a ballboy at the Eagles training camp that summer. Rita tells him he hasn't gotten home from training camp. "No, I want Joe Senior." I get up to take the call and Leonard tells me "You go the job. Report on Monday." He went on to explain to me that he took a helicopter down to Atlantic City, met with Weinberger and Rosen and informed them that if they didn't hire me he was never setting foot in Bally's again. When I went down to meet with Al Rosen, he told me that the interview had gone well and I was going to get the job anyway, but I have no doubt that the threat of Leonard Tose parking his limo in front of another casino helped influence the decision.

I can't say enough about Leonard Tose and what he meant to me and my family.

I remember reading articles about him where he was quoted as saying that he wasn't sure how many millions he lost gambling in Atlantic City. When someone asked him if it was true that he lost $14 million at the Sands, he answered, "Fourteen million? Oh, it was more than that. I think it was more than $20 million at Resorts. Fourteen was the number at the Sands. I don't even know what the total number was for sure. I don't want to know about the losses." Leonard did everything for me. Whenever he came into Bally's he made it clear that he wouldn't play unless I was there to draw the markers for him. He did it all for me. I remember the night he spotted Lynn Revson, who had been married to Revlon founder Charles Revson. She was wearing a too-tight gold dress and Leonard's eyes popped out of his head when he saw her. He said he had to meet her and they started dating. Leonard didn't need any intermediaries. He went over, introduced himself, 'Hello, I'm Leonard Tose'; and with that they became an item. He'd call her and she'd book a dinner at the swankiest restaurants in New York. She told me that Leonard would have his driver pull the car right up on the sidewalk at the front door, hand the doorman $100 and tell him to take care of the car. Leonard was a special person and he helped me get established at Bally's, which turned out to be the best possible place for me to get a start in the casino business.

Getting hired did not bring an immediate end to my frustrations as there was some ongoing aggravation after I took the job. I had dutifully filled out all of the applications to get my casino license but then things dragged on for much longer that I anticipated. I don't think it's much of a reach to believe that the extra delay was a direct result of having an Italian last name. No one would publicly admit it, but it was quietly acknowledged that the state gaming people were concerned about keeping mob-related types out of the casinos. I had this discussion with Bob Pellegrini when he was also sweating out this prolonged delay in getting his license. I went to Billy Weinberger and told him this was bullshit, I'm squeaky clean; there's nothing to dig up. Billy told me to calm down, but I was hot. I wanted to get my new job started and also reminded him that I had a wife and four kids. I was stomping around threatening to send a letter claiming discrimination against my Italian heritage. I composed the letter and had every intention of mailing it out if I didn't hear back by the end of the week. Two days later, I received my license. Las Vegas was still cleaning itself up from the years of mob infiltration and, because people were so afraid of history repeating itself in Atlantic City, it was extra tough for an Italian to get a decent casino job in the 70's and early 80's.

Quite simply, in my estimation, Billy Weinberger was the smartest casino boss in Atlantic City. He didn't necessarily know the East Coast market, but he lived by one basic rule: develop your base around quality high rollers and then take care of them; don't give them a reason to leave. Billy was also smart enough to take care of the wives. The wives were important, most of them knew that their husbands visited the casino, but very few of the high rollers wanted their spouses to know how much they were losing. If the guy brought home a nice watch, expensive piece of jewelry or designer perfume after a rough night, the wife was less likely to grill him about how much he lost. We had the greatest gift room at Bally's. The room was heavily secured, but if you had to take care of a high roller, you could go in and sign out an expensive gift. When warranted, we even reached outside the gift room. In one instance, I had a brand-new Mercedes-Benz delivered for a special high roller.

Billy also recognized that even the most successful and accomplished high rollers could melt like 10-year olds when they were shaking hands with big-time athletes. Al Rosen was a good and smart man, but there is no doubt that Billy brought him in because he had been a well-known major league baseball player. It was Billy, along with Al, who developed the Bally's Sports Legends program and they didn't use the term 'Legend' lightly. They had Willie Mays on the payroll and, in addition, they brought in names like Ernie Banks, Bob Feller, Bob Gibson, Brooks Robinson, Al Kaline, Frank Robinson, Warren Spahn, Rick Barry, Elgin Baylor, Bob Cousy, Julius Erving, Walt Frazier, Oscar Robertson, Chuck Bednarik, Otto Graham, Lenny Moore, Gale Sayers, Jim Taylor, Johnny Unitas, Joe Frazier, Larry Holmes, Gordie Howe, Bobby Hull, Phil Esposito, Rafer Johnson and Mark Spitz. I doubt that there has ever been a lineup like that presented anywhere.

Billy Weinberger validated everything Al Besseslink had always preached to me, mainly that the key to success in this business was to do anything within the law to take care of your best customers. Deliver to them things they didn't even know they might need or want. About the only thing we were prohibited from procuring was female companionship. If someone was dropping enough money with us, we could arrange for anything: tickets to shows, sports events, dinner, limos, helicopters, golf, sports memorabilia, you name it. Anything that is, but sex.

Billy was my mentor. We would ride around Atlantic City together, go to the race-track, have dinner. Atlantic City was really beat up once you stepped away from the boardwalk. All the conversations at the time were about how the city was going to be redeveloped around the casinos and hotels, but thirty-five years later it doesn't seem like much has happened. There were big plans for the future of Atlantic City with as many as 12 casinos generating money and pumping so much of it back into the surrounding area. The Casino Reinvestment Development Authority was set up by the State of New Jersey to distribute a portion of the casino-generated funds into the overall improvement of the area. Supposedly CRDA spent something like $1.5 billion on Atlantic City projects, but I can't see where most of that money went. For a while things were definitely turning around, then progress seemed to come to a stop. I go down there now and the area still looks pretty much the same. The old timers that I know bitch about how high their the taxes are and they're still continuing to skyrocket. Billy used to tell me as we were driving around that once I started making money I should invest in Atlantic City real estate, that's one of the few pieces of his advice that I'm glad that I never followed.

Real estate advice aside, I learned so much from Billy. He knew how to talk to anybody. In addition to the people inside the casino world, Billy was great dealing with the surrounding community. All the casinos were new at that time and Billy always understood the importance of making as many friends as possible. He was friendly with all of the politicians, civic groups, business people and community leaders. He was also always active with charity and religious groups. As sharp as he was as a casino executive, he was just as much a genuine humanitarian. I was getting an advanced education watching him interact with people.

For Bally's it was a coup bringing Billy to Atlantic City, he brought with him instant class and credibility. He was held in as high regard as anyone in the casino industry. In 1979 Bally's Park Place became the third casino to open in Atlantic City and, within about a year, it had the highest cash flow of any of the gaming halls. This trend would continue for years thereafter. Billy was a classic street person, he didn't have traditional come-up-through-the-ranks formal training, but he had innate smarts. As far as I know, he was the guy who introduced the 'Black Book,' the little black notebook that you carried around and wrote down everything about your players. I still have my original black books, the ones that were inspired by Billy. He taught me how to be a casino executive. One of Billy's gifts was that he had an eye for recognizing hard work and dedicated effort and he had a reputation for promoting and giving more responsibility to people who put out and earned it. If you were willing to work hard and work smart, it wouldn't escape Billy's attention and he would find opportunities to move you up within the organization. There were countless stories of people who worked their way up from entry level to executive positions. I remember one local woman that was hired for some basic administrative job: she was smart and personable and worked her way up to become head of human resources. There was no better person in the industry for me to begin my casino career with than Billy.

Billy had been brought out to oversee the construction and he was involved in every last detail. He knew how to lay out a casino. Most casino floors may look pretty much the same, but I saw some monumental design mistakes during my time in Atlantic City. We were all invited over when the Playboy Club opened up and we had to take an escalator or elevator up to the fourth or fifth floor to get to the gaming floor. I remember thinking to myself that people aren't going to travel this far to gamble. It was an especially tough ride after you lost. Playboy lasted in the business about three years and went into bankruptcy. The property re-emerged as the Atlantis Hotel and Casino, then Donald Trump bought in and turned it into Trump Regency and later Trump World's Fair. One night when Trump was operating it, some pissed off gambler jammed the buttons on all of the elevators and the cars were getting stalled with people inside them and those outside were stranded on their floors; it was an ugly night. The property eventually closed for good and was torn down in 2000. This was one gambling hall that never stood a chance, doomed from the start by its design.

I learned something from Billy every day, not just about the casino business, but life in general. One of the early lessons I picked up was to never attach your name when you made any kind of donation. My first year on the job, I chipped in with a few co-workers to buy some holiday dinners for a few local families. We all signed the card. Next thing, I'm getting hit for a donation from every imaginable group. I mentioned this to Billy and he scolded me, "You never put your name on anything. These lists all get shared and everybody's going to be after you with their hand out. It's okay to help, but do it 'from a friend.'"

Billy was legend in the industry before arriving in Atlantic City. He had been working in his family's catering business when he took a job as food and beverage manager at Caesar's Palace when it opened on the Las Vegas Strip in 1966. Two years later he was president and Caesar's was renowned as the preferred gaming spot for high rollers, celebrities, foreign dignitaries and wise guys. When he came to Atlantic City he was able to bring a lot of these people with him, especially those on the East Coast who had been flying to Vegas to satisfy their gaming pleasures. As I continued to work my ass off and gain Billy's confidence, many of these same people would get turned over to me.

Billy Weinberger was one of the few people who had a plan. Most of the casino executives in the early years of Atlantic City were just learning on the job and winging it, I don't think there was an overall mindset other than 'let's make a lot of money.'

Every single day I tried my damndest to be the best casino host in the business. I followed the advice of Al Besselink and Billy Weinberger and neatly logged every last detail about every high roller in one of my black books. As soon as I filled up one book, I started another. Every morning I checked the lists of the 10 highest winners and 10 highest losers from the previous day and added that info to my books. I became friendly with the operators in our phone room and told them, "You get any difficult calls, turn them over to me." I wanted to know everything about all of the key players and kept track of birthdays, names of spouse and kids, where they came from and favorite restaurants. Some of the guys sponsored charity golf tournaments at their local country clubs: we would buy a foursome and make some kind of donation. I stayed on top of everything and kept it to myself, hidden in my personal black books.

I made sure that I stayed close to the marketing people and I always wanted to know in advance about the events they had planned, who they might be bringing in. The more advance notice I had, the more thought I could give to which of my high rollers I wanted to invite. If a particular entertainer was coming to town and I had a high roller (or wife) who was a fan, I would invite them before the appearance was even made public. I wanted them to think I was doing something special for them. I strived to earn the confidence of everyone at Bally's and make them aware that I was the guy who could deliver the biggest and best return for their investment. It got to the point where I expected to have someone from the executive office call me and say, "Joe, we have this big event coming up. We'd like you be there to take care of the guests."

I picked up early that if you wanted to be a successful host, the most important attribute was personality. You had to be personable and comfortable around people. Sounds obvious, but some hosts never picked up on that. You had people who simply were not nice or gave off a 'that's not my problem' attitude. As for me, it wasn't difficult to find empathy for gamblers and I had Clairton to thank for that, I grew up watching people lose their money. I saw how a guy like Moe Martin never gloated when a player was having a rough night. He might even slip a few bucks back so that the guy might at least be able to bring something home for dinner.

I loved the business from the first night I stepped on the floor as a host. I recognized a lot of faces from my years hanging out at the track and knew this was where I belonged. Everything about being around a casino fascinated me. I didn't want to leave the floor. They used to close up all the casinos at 2 am and I would just hang around. The cleaning crews would attack the floor like an army, with golf carts scooting all around to pick up trash. They'd roll their scissor lifts in and guys would be going up and down cleaning the lights.

I got to know everything about my players. It was especially important to be there for them when they lost big, you never wanted to see a guy go home having lost everything. The least I would try to do was make sure they didn't leave hungry, it wasn't too much of a stretch for a player to not even have enough for a hamburger when he left the gambling floor. One of the things about the casinos is that nearly all of them have great food. Big-time attention is given to getting the right chefs, menus and the whole dining experience. I'd catch a guy leaving the floor having lost everything, and I'd say, "Let me make a reservation and buy you dinner."

One of my players was getting ready to go home after a particularly tough night and I told him I'd buy him dinner. I asked what he was in the mood for and he hesitates for a moment and answers, "Calamari…I could go for some black calamari." I called over to our restaurant and they didn't have any calamari in stock. I told my high roller we didn't have it that night, "But next time you come in, I'll buy you a calamari dinner." The next day the kitchen orders 60 pounds of calamari and I said, "What the hell are you going to do with 60 pounds? I wanted to buy one guy dinner." They ended up freezing it and any time this guy came in he had calamari waiting for him.

I had learned straight from Billy Weinberger the importance of never letting a guy go home hungry. During my first year at Bally's I got a call from one of our heavy hitters. He had lost something like $50,000 that night and wanted to get a steak dinner before driving home. He goes to the casino restaurant and the maître d' tells him they are booked solid, "Look at the line to get in, we have nothing open." I get the call, this guy is furious. He just dropped a load of cash at our tables and he can't get a table in our restaurant. I called Billy and asked what to do. He tells me take the guy around back, walk him in, have a table set up in the dining room and tell the waiter give the guy anything he wanted. I didn't even know where the back of the restaurant was, but I take the guy in and he was so appreciative that I made the effort for him. The next day Billy fired the maître d'.

Some guys just can't listen, especially when they are ahead. I had a restaurant owner from New York, Pasquale, who used to come down and play. One night he was up $100,000 and I told him to take his money and get the hell out of here. He said, "No, no, I'm on a roll; I'm gonna break this place." I see him a couple of hours later and he lost everything.

Personally, the heaviest of my hitters was Ahmad Hussein of Kuwait. He showed up at the casino unannounced on the Thursday of a Fourth of July weekend and left $1.5 million poorer. The hotel was sold out for the weekend and I got a call from the front desk asking me to come down and meet someone. Waiting for me was a gentleman in a Jungle Jim safari outfit, asking what it would take to get a couple of suites for the weekend. I told him that we had some suites in reserve that were being held for big players. He handed me three books of American Express Travelers Checks, each containing $500,000. That got him his rooms. I asked when he wanted to start playing and he said he would be down in about a half hour. I took his money and placed it in the cage, went to one of the roulette tables, had it roped off and told them that this would be $5,000 minimum bet. The floor manager told me I was crazy, they couldn't do that. I said, "Just do it." The manager calls Billy Weinberger and tells him that him that "Pags is out of his mind." Billy gets me on the phone and says, "You crazy son of a bitch, we have a packed floor, do you know what you're doing?" I told him, "Trust me, I landed a whale." He's yelling into the phone, "Bullshit, bullshit." I calmly told him to go to his computer and take notice that $1.5 million had been deposited in the last hour. Billy looked it up, but still not comfortable, told me that I had better be right, that if I was wrong I was out of here. I had the balls to ask him what he would do if I was right. He answered that we would talk about that later.

It took Ahmad a couple of days to burn through that bankroll. The morning of his departure, I went up to his room and he greeted me in a robe that he said was his native garb back home. I asked him what we could do for him, we'd like to buy him a gift, and he said he would like a Mercedes-Benz convertible. I called Billy and asked if that was okay, and he said, "Give it to him." I told Ahmad that we couldn't have it before he left, but would have it for the next time he came in. I called up Kerbeck, a luxury car dealer in the area and they said they could deliver a powder blue Mercedes with a white top, but it would take three weeks. I relayed that message to Ahmad and we had it ready for him when he came back.

He comes in a few weeks later and we had the car waiting for him in front of the hotel with a gift card signed by Billy Weinberger, Al Rosen and myself. Ahmad checked in and proceeded to drop another $750,000 in about 24 hours. Again, I asked what we could do for him and he said he could use a watch. We sent him over to our jewelry store and he picked out seven Rolex watches, costing about $8,000 each. Ahmad was grateful and invited me to visit him in Kuwait, adding that I could bring along anyone I wanted. I called Billy Weinberger and told him we were going to Kuwait, he replied, "Joe, Jews don't go to Kuwait." Don't know what happened to him, but we never saw Ahmad Hussein again after that. Hussein's visits earned me a small bonus. Billy was so appreciative that he covered all of my moving expenses from Pennsauken to Northfield and gave me the guarantee of a lifetime job.

There were also those high rollers who could place you in a difficult spot. While we, as hosts, never got involved in the procurement of women, there were ladies of the night who plied their trade in and around the casinos. One of my players had the balls to stiff his date for that night and lock her in his hotel bathroom while he dressed and slipped off of the premises. He did not take into consideration that most of the bathrooms in Bally's were equipped with telephones. The hooker called down to the front desk screaming about what that Mr. X had just done to her and security went up, got her out and told her to get dressed and leave the property. I was called over and as I'm standing outside the room she comes out with a bedspread, clock radio and a pillow. We asked her what she thought she was doing and she said, "That son-of-a-bitch stiffed me and I'm getting paid somehow."

We did our best to keep hookers off the property, but they were pretty inventive. We'd catch them on the floor and throw them out. We found out that for some reason a lot of them were coming from Pittsburgh. One of them hustled one of my high rollers and few weeks later he was back at the casino with his wife. He saw the hooker and was nervous that she was going to come up to him, so he alerted security and they threw her out. Security called me because my guy had reported her and I was watching as they walked her out. Two weeks later she was back in the casino as a redhead. I recognized her face and told her she better get out of here before I called security and had her thrown out again.

Billy Weinberger had come into Atlantic City with a 'we can get anybody' attitude. As I progressed in the business and these bigger 'gets' were handed over to me, I developed a similar confidence. Later, I remember telling Tommy Lasorda when we were putting together a roast for him that we could 'get' anybody we wanted to show up for the event.

Billy was the first to introduce a big name former athlete as a casino host in Atlantic City. This was a practice that had been utilized in Las Vegas, but no one tried it in AC until 1979, when Billy gave Willie Mays a $100,000 a year contract to hang out with the gamblers, pose for photos, sign autographs, and maybe play some golf. Other casinos would follow suit, even though the May's signing created something of a controversy. At the time, Willie was working as a consultant with the New York Mets and, because of his association with a casino, Major League Baseball Commissioner Bowie Kuhn forced him to sever all ties with professional baseball.

For me, Willie's association with Bally's and his love for golf proved to be my first big break in the business. Barely one week into the job, Bally's needed a host to accompany Willie on his golf outings with high rollers. Because I knew my way around the links, from that day on, I was Willie Mays' designated travelling companion any time he made an appearance on behalf of Bally's. I got to meet a lot of people by tagging along with Willie.

Billy Weinberger returned to Las Vegas in 1988, going to work for the Golden Nugget and later, The Mirage. We continued to stay in touch and the last time I saw him was when I was working at Harrah's in the early 1990's. He called to say that he was coming in from Vegas and asked if I could send a car to meet him. I told him, "Hell, I'll send a helicopter." He came into the casino, asked for a $10,000 marker, lost it all in about 10 minutes, stopped by to chat a little more and then left. He died in 1996.

Having grown up around gambling in Clairton and then spending so much time around racetracks, I thought there was little that could surprise me when it came to gamblers, but I was constantly being introduced to new firsts at Bally's. One day I got a call that there is a guy who is running his own personal loan shark operation outside one of the money cages. Seems this guy from Philly would take out a $10,000 marker and, rather than gamble, he had his own system for making money. He'd stand off to the side of the cage and keep an eye out for people who came looking for markers, but couldn't get one because of bad credit. Once they were turned down, this guy would pull them aside and offer $1000 for a $1200 payback. He was operating a payday loan-operation right under our noses. I went over, caught him, cancelled his credit line and threw him out. A few weeks later I'm walking through the casino and a hand reaches over and grabs me from behind by the shoulder and says "You're the son-of-a-bitch who shut me down. I was just trying to help people, you cancelled my credit and now I'm out of business." I told him, "You're not helping anybody lending out our money at 6-5. You're lucky I don't knock you out." Nice operation he had: borrow our money, lend it out to someone we turned down, and make an easy 20% return.

Then there was the guy who turned a trip to the bathroom into a payday. Slots weren't the only place in Bally's where you could deposit a quarter, we also had pay toilet stalls in the restrooms. One player lost all of his money on the floor and had to borrow a quarter from me to use the facility. I didn't have any change so I gave him a dollar which he broke into change and went into the restroom. Someone was leaving a stall as he walked in, so he grabbed the door before it shut, didn't spend anything and left with four quarters in his pocket. While exiting the casino floor he put the four quarters into a slot and kept winning until he walked out with $1000. The guy came back to tell me the story and thank me.

When you work at a casino, you show up for work every day with the awareness that everything you do is being watched. Bally's, like every other casino, had the 'eye-in-the-sky' closed circuit cameras that monitored everywhere, not only the gaming floor, but lobbies, hallways, restaurants and elevators. In addition, we had a catwalk surrounding the perimeter of the floor and it was manned by a troop of Korean War veterans who were trained in observation. They would patrol the catwalk and, when they got a signal from someone on the floor or up in the observation room, they'd train binoculars and zero in on the suspected party. None of the casinos like parting with their money, but they don't mind legitimate losses. They know they have to give some-thing back, but they do not like to be cheated.

The first time I saw security in action was when a guy was picked up cheating at the Craps table. Security cuffed him and dragged him down to what was known as the 'sweat room' in the basement. It was located right off the side of the employee cafeteria, so whenever someone was dragged in there it was visible to all the casino workers who were dining at the time. We wanted the employees to be aware whenever we caught a cheater. Our guys would quiz them hard about how they were cheating and whether they were working with anyone on the inside. We needed to know if any of our employees were involved. In reality, the casino was more interested in getting information than in pursuing prosecution. They wanted to know everything about how the person was cheating and, after the grilling, they would ban the cheater from the premises and tell them if there was a next time the police would be brought in.

One guy got caught cheating at Blackjack. Four security guards cuffed him behind the back and started walking him off the floor. He was mouthing off all the way and as they pushed him forward he tripped and landed flush on his face, bleeding all over the place. They took him into the sweat room, cleaned him up and literally threw him through an exit door with the threat (or promise) that things would only get worse if he ever showed up again.

We had signs posted around the gaming floor that could conveniently be uncovered or hidden, depending on the circumstances of the moment. They were relatively small signs that addressed the right to deny a player the opportunity to continue if they were winning too much or we suspected something might not be right. The signs simply read: "WE RESERVE THE RIGHT TO NOT INCLUDE ANY PLAYER IN A GAME." The wording was non-specific enough to give us the leeway to evict a player who was causing some degree of discomfort for the house.

Looking back, I would have to say that the real cheaters, the good ones, never got caught. Our focus was more on the people who tried to cheat, but didn't really know how, or just didn't do it well enough.

Sometimes you can be too close to the action to see things clearly. For as scrutinizing and precise as our security people tried to be, there were some things they just couldn't pick up. We were constantly getting beat on the second game of 21, right near the dealer's cage. One night an executive from one of the other casinos, I think it was the Claridge, was on our floor and he picked right up on what the problem was, called us over and had us watch what was going on. The way we were set up, all of the odd number games were played with blue decks of cards, the even games had red cards. In this instance, our second game was being played with blue cards. We watched this live and when we checked the security tapes, we saw this was going on nearly every night. The pit boss would drop a full shoe of blue cards on the table. We had been getting beat on this table, for as much as a couple of hundred grand a night, too often. When we confronted the pit boss, he dumbed himself down and claimed everything was accidental and unintentional. Of course we didn't believe him, he would have his own players come in and sit at this table.

Sometimes it seems that everybody on a casino payroll is looking for a way to get in on a scam. We eventually picked up that even the hotel front desk workers had a quiet little racket going. In was common for us to comp a suite to a high roller for the entire weekend. Say they checked in Friday, lost all their money and went home Saturday. Well, the front desk people kept their own private lists of players who were on the lookout for a discounted room. The desk person would call this other party, or maybe their own friend or relative, and tell them that they could get them a nice price on suite for that night, provided they paid cash. Of course the cash was pocketed, the room registration never changed, and whoever moved into the suite had full food and beverage access under the name of Mr. and Mrs. Comped High Roller. They would be instructed to just say, "Lou Brown," and anything they wanted was on the house. Eventually this was busted and hotel workers came under the same scrutiny as Blackjack dealers.

I was doing well for myself at Bally's and, at that time in my life, was prepared to stay there forever. I had earned so much confidence and respect that when the top brass had to designate someone to meet with a prospective high roller from New York, I was the person selected. This meeting would lead to another life changing experience and I would find myself working side-by-side with a future President of the United States.

*With Julius Erving
(right) at his Roast*

Guess who's back at Bally's?

*Charo and me
at the Roast*

*Willie Mays
and Joe Pagliei*

Here I am rubbing elbows with Tommy Lasorda (center) and Bobby Rydell

With friends Mike Mathews, Mayor of Atlantic City, standing on my left and seated: Leo Durocher (left) and Willie Mays

8 – DONALD TRUMP AND HARRAHS

I can now state, from this time forward, that I was hired personally by the future President of the United States. In fact, to the best of my knowledge, I was the only person hired by Donald Trump himself when he opened and operated his first Atlantic City casino. I have little doubt that Donald would have entered the casino business whether or not he met me, but I am the proud possessor of the first brain he picked when he was thinking of entering the AC scene, was his first hire, and was the first guy that he always asked for whenever he was onsite.

It all started when my boss at Bally's asked me to go and have lunch with this rich real estate guy from New York and maybe get him to come over and be one of our heavy hitter players. When I met Donald for the first time, I had no knowledge that he was looking to get into the casino business himself.

Richard Gilman was the CEO of Bally's Place and he called me into his office one morning in 1982 to inform me that I would be having lunch with someone named Donald Trump at the deli at Bally's. Fred Trump, Donald's father, was the better known member of the family at that time and Richard told me that they were prominent in New York real estate. Rita recalls me saying that I told her I was going to meet with some 'kids from New York who were in real estate.' The original meeting was supposed to be with Donald and his brother Robert. Billy Weinberger had always taught me that for a big meeting, to reserve the middle table in a restaurant and always follow 'Lombardi Time,' as in Vince Lombardi, and that meant showing up 15 minutes early.

This was all happening well before the days of the cell phone and, at the time, I always had to be near a telephone in order to take calls from my high rollers who might be showing up that night and wanted to reserve something for that evening—an increased credit line, room, meal—or maybe just wanted to let me know they were coming in. I called ahead to the deli manager and had a table set up with a phone.

I'm seated at the center table with a phone in front of me and at 12 noon sharp, Donald Trump walks into the restaurant. He was alone that first meeting. I had tipped off the manager to make a fuss over him, which he did as he escorted him to my table. I probably made somewhat of a big shot impression, parked in the center of the restaurant with the phone ringing every other minute. I kept apologizing to Donald for all for the interruptions, but in hindsight I don't know if anything else could have made a bigger or better first impression. I explained to Donald that I was a credit executive, and it was credit that kept our most important players coming back. How it was they, in turn, who made the most money for the casino. I would tell Donald a little about the backgrounds of each player who called and he'd hear me talking about how much credit would be in play for that night.

Between phone calls, Donald was asking me questions about the casino operation. He was asking more probing questions than the typical prospective player, but I had no indication that he was looking to get into the operational end of the business. He did make it clear that he was in real estate and construction and might have an interest

80

in building a casino. I would soon learn that Donald Trump always had a plan and, looking back, there is no uncertainty in my mind that he walked into that first lunch with an idea of owning and operating his own casino. That interest only heightened as he eavesdropped on my phone conversations and absorbed the dollar amounts that were casually getting tossed around.

After lunch I gave him a tour of the casino and explained the different aspects of the operation. Billy Weinberger was as good a pro as there was in the casino business and he had done everything right in the design of Bally's. Plus Bally's enjoyed the benefit of prime real estate, located at the famed intersection of "Boardwalk and Park Place," the most prized Monopoly properties. Donald still hadn't made any inference to getting into the business, but as he left he shook my hand and said, "I might be giving you a call to come work for me someday."

My thoughts about Donald after that first meeting? He didn't say or do anything to come off as a know-it-all. I did most of the talking. He asked intelligent questions and came off as a very bright guy; he was likable and low-key.

I went back to the office and told Richard Gilman that I didn't think this guy held any potential as a high roller, and pretty much forgot about him. I had no contact, did not hear anything from Donald for more than a year. One day I get a phone call and Donald Trump is on the other end. He tells me that he is sending two of his vice presidents down to Atlantic City and would like me to meet with them and to be prepared to tell them how much money I would want to go to work for him.

I set it up to meet with Donald's two guys at the diner over in Somers Point and also had one of my regular racquetball sessions with Richard Gilman set for that afternoon. As he usually did, Richard sent a car and driver to pick me up. I told the driver that I had to make a stop on the way to the courts, so I pull up to my meeting with the Trump executives wearing a warm-up suit in a chauffeur-driven car. I didn't think anything of the imagery at the time, but now in this post-Sopranos era, I have to laugh when I think about that first impression: an Italian guy sets a meeting at a New Jersey diner and shows up wearing a designer warm up suit with a personal driver.

During the year-plus since our initial meeting, there had been absolutely no buzz, whispers or rumors in the air that Donald Trump was thinking of getting into the casino business. I walked into the diner and opened by telling the Trump guys that this was going to be short and sweet, I'm on my way to meet the Chairman of the Board of Bally's and you guys can't pay me enough to come and work for you. I threw a number out at them, and they gasped and told me I was crazy, that even they didn't make that kind of money. I felt like I was a winner either way. I wasn't anxious to leave Bally's, but if they met my asking price, I'd listen. Either way was fine with me.

I go on to my racquetball game and then to work. At home that night, my phone rings and again, it's Donald Trump on the other end. He tells me that he needs me and is going to meet my asking price. My reaction was "Oh, shit." I didn't think the Trump guys had taken me seriously and I wasn't prepared for this. I loved working at Bally's.

The first call I made was to Billy Weinberger to ask, "What do I do?"

Billy told me to take the offer, that I had to do what was best for my family and that there was no way he could match it. He added that if things didn't work out, I could always come back; he'd always have a place for me.

I called Donald Trump and told him that I would be going to work for him. I went up to New York to meet with him, we shook hands and he handed me a hard hat, telling me that he needed me on the job immediately.

I turned around, went right back to Atlantic City, hard hat in hand, and reported to the Harrah's at Trump Plaza construction site. I was there on the job as the walls went up and the floors went in. Harrah's was already operating a casino at the Marina and they had been looking to expand in Atlantic City. The company was then owned by Holiday Inn and had been a longtime fixture in Las Vegas. I later learned that some of their executives had gone to New York to meet with the Trump family to discuss the possibility of having them build a new Harrah's casino in Atlantic City. The Harrah's people explained that they were looking for a unique design and to date were not happy with anything that had been presented. In one of the conference rooms they saw some casino renderings that Donald had designed. The Harrah's reps got excited and said that was exactly what they were looking for. Donald told them that building was off limits, he had it designed for his company as they might be looking to get into in the business at some point. That got the discussions started about a potential Harrah's/ Trump partnership.

Harrah's had come to New York for that first meeting to discuss having the Trumps build their casino. When the meetings ended, the Trumps were their partners. Not only was Donald paid to build the casino, he was to receive an equal share of the profits and was amortized from operational losses for the first five years. Donald Trump was in the casino business.

Harrah's at Trump Plaza opened May 15, 1984. Built at a cost $210 million, it became the 10th and largest casino in Atlantic City. I was on the Harrah's payroll, but I had been hired by Donald and, for the most part, he was who I reported to.

About a week after I went to work for Donald, he called me and said he was sending his father down by helicopter and wanted me to meet him and give him the full tour. I prepared myself for the meeting, making sure I knew every last detail: how many rooms, how many tables, number of employees, you name it. I ordered a limo, met Fred at Bader Airport, showed him the complex and gave a tour of Atlantic City. The whole time Fred is talking about how smart his kid was, how beautiful the design was, look at how this place is being constructed, it's going to be the greatest casino in the world, he couldn't believe the view of the ocean. He thought that it was brilliant that Donald had included a walkway to Convention Hall so you could go directly back and forth between whatever event was going on there and our casino.

I took Fred back to Bader and we wished each other well. I get back to my office and get a call from the limo driver that Fred had left his wallet in the backseat of the car. I told him to lock it up for safekeeping. A little while later I get a call from Donald, telling me that his father lost his wallet. I told him don't worry we have it. Donald sent the chopper back down to Atlantic City, with no one aboard but the pilot. I picked up the wallet, put it in a brown paper bag, met the chopper at Bader and sent it on its way back to New York. Both Donald and Fred called to thank me.

Fred was a very quiet, easygoing guy. A smile would come to his face every time he talked about his son. I would spend some time with Fred during my association with Harrah's at Trump Plaza and it didn't take long to recognize that his favorite topic of conversation was his son Donald. Nothing wrong with that I guess, a parent taking pride in the accomplishments of their kid.

Of course I had brought my black books of high rollers with me to Harrah's. I gave them to the computer operators and they produced these master lists that included everything about the players, credit lines, where they lived, family info, every detail I had come up with. I ended up with over 3,000 names of people who could win or lose $10,000 or more in a sitting and I had about another 1,000 names of smaller players. When I was at Bally's I wrote down every name I could get access to and now, for the first time, I had everything computerized. Most of my important players followed me to Harrah's at Trump Plaza.

Joe Pagliei Jr. was never surprised by the loyalty his father engendered with his players, and appreciated it even more when he himself became an executive casino host:

"My dad helped me get set up as a host and helped me build my casino customer base. He had a very big following. He was different than most casino hosts in that he really cared about his players and never tried to take advantage of them. Our family saw a lot of people we knew lose their homes, their businesses, their marriages, because of gambling. My dad would never encourage people to play for more than they could handle. He might have someone ask him, 'Joe what do I have to do get a suite or a steak dinner?' He would tell them, 'Do you really want to lose $5,000 just for a free dinner; why don't you take $150 out of the bank and take your wife for a real nice night out?'"

Somewhat surprisingly, I never had any second thoughts about leaving Bally's. Donald made me feel valued from the start. When all of the construction was completed, Donald took me down to the parking garage below the building, it was one of these New York-style elaborately ramped structures. We're driving around and around on these ramps and when we get to the executive parking area, Donald points to the third spot, right next to the two that were reserved for him, and tells me that's my space. Donald always treated me with respect and took first class care of me.

Just prior to the grand opening we were going to have a party up in the suites on the top floor that were reserved for the high rollers. Donald had designed the suites and they were as nice as any in town; he knew exactly what he wanted. He had me take his wife at the time, Ivana, around to see them. She went crazy. She didn't like the way they looked, didn't like the fixtures or the colors. In one suite she ordered what must have been about $200,000 worth of marble ripped out.

LeRoy Neiman, the famous artist was another who wasn't impressed with the suites. Shortly after we opened, I was hanging around at the front desk and Neiman came down complaining about his suite. He said he didn't like it at all and that he was checking out and never coming back. I went over introduced myself and said I'd find something else that suited him. We went back up on the elevator, I showed him the different suites, he picked out one that he was happy with and we went on to become great friends. I have a portrait that he painted of me wearing my red Trump power tie. When Donald made it known that he preferred red ties, everyone around the casino started wearing them. It seemed that every damned guy in the place would be wearing a red tie when they knew Donald was coming in. LeRoy would go on to design the invitations and programs for golf outings and roasts that I would host at the casino.

The relationship between Donald and Harrah's seemed okay during its infancy, but as time wore on, and not very much time at that, maybe three, four, six months, we started getting indications from Donald and his people that they were unhappy with the way Harrah's was operating. Donald had evolved from builder to silent partner to not-so-silent partner. This was also around the time that Donald was emerging as a regular topic of coverage in the New York media. You could tell that his personal celebrity was growing, each time he came down to visit more people would recognize him. We would be taking our walks around the casino floor and the players would wave at him and yell "Hey Donald, how ya' doing." He would usually answer, "Fine, I hope you lose all of your money."

When Donald was onsite, word would spread that he had arrived and he usually wasn't happy. There were issues about the casino name. Donald thought the Trump name should be more prominent and would be a better marketing tool for attracting high rollers. This is the mid-1980's and 'Trump' was now flashing all across New York: newspapers, radio, television. Donald was becoming increasingly aware of the branding power attached to his name and he also wanted 'Harrah's' dropped entirely from the project, claiming it caused confusion with the Harrah's Marina site. Donald further enflamed the relationship in 1985 when he opened Trump's Castle and Casino, and now Harrah's did not want Donald to have HIS name on a competitive property. Less than a year-and-a-half after opening, the partners of Harrah's at Trump Plaza were sitting on opposite sides of a courtroom.

In defense of Donald, Harrah's had brought a lot of people in from Las Vegas and they really didn't understand how things were done on the East Coast. Harrah's came into New Jersey with about 40-years of experience operating casinos in Nevada. They were set in their ways. Donald was looking to operate at a more grandiose level. One of his quotes at the time was, "I gave them a Lamborghini and they didn't know how to turn on the key." I think the best way to put it was that Atlantic City was attracting a more sophisticated clientele than Vegas was used to. The difference around the slot machines might not be noticeable, but in those days the table games accounted for about 85% of the gaming revenue, and our high rollers were showing up dressed for a night out on the town. Vegas featured a much more casual atmosphere. If someone was winning at one of our tables, the Harrah's bosses would change the dealer as they were taught to do in Vegas, and our customers wouldn't put up with the type of stuff. In Atlantic City we tried to treat people with class, in Vegas and Reno, they pretty much just opened the doors.

Both Harrah's and my former employer, Bally's, had come into Atlantic City with established Nevada pedigrees, yet different operational standards.

The biggest difference between the two approaches?

Honestly, I would have to say Billy Weinberger. Harrah's lacked a visionary with Billy's style. The Harrah's gang was made up of competent gaming people, but they operated more like stewards; what worked in Vegas or Reno would also work in New Jersey. Donald Trump, the ultimate New Yorker, was always looking to looking to elevate things to a royal level. Billy understood that you had to adapt to your market.

Over at Bally's, Billy was the one casino boss in Atlantic City who was always thinking two steps ahead of the curve. Those who are old enough to have lived through it will remember those dreaded days of gas shortages, with all the rationing and long lines. Bally's bought a gas station so that we would never lose a high roller because he couldn't get gas. We always made sure we had enough gas on hand for our car service so that we would be able to send a car to pick up a high roller. This also put us in a position to send a player home with a full tank of gas after a rough night at the tables. Bally's also bought some warehouses offshore in places like Pleasantville so that we could keep our limos stored and cleaned. Bally's was also the major player in the manufacturing of slot machines and we always had an inventory of parts on hand to make a quick repair. Bally's was not going to allow a slot machine to be down for an extended period because parts had to be ordered. From a family perspective, it was also handy having a connection in the gaming machine business. One year my kids were looking for a pinball machine for our basement. I mentioned it to the chairman, Richard Gilman, and his only questions were where and when I wanted it delivered. For a very nominal fee, a pinball machine was delivered and set up in our house.

I think another issue that might have hindered the Harrah's operation was that, by the time we opened, most of the really good people were already working in the established casinos, and if they were doing well they weren't anxious to leave. Remember, Harrah's at Trump Plaza was the 10th casino to open in Atlantic City and the pool of quality workers was drying up. We were almost like a new expansion team, getting the leftover players that nobody else wanted. Harrah's was good to me and I was pretty much left to run free and manage my own operation. I was, by far, bringing in more big players than anyone else and my authority increased as I continued to produce.

Atlantic City was opening up a lot of eyes in the casino industry with all of these private planes and choppers and limos coming in and out. Our slowest casinos were taking in more than the best performers in Vegas. Sadly, that era was short-lived. Within about 10-12 years the tables-to-slots ratios flipped completely around and by the mid-90's slots were providing 85% of the action and were taking up more space on the gaming floors as the number of table players shrunk. What I saw happen with my players list was prevalent throughout AC. I had a pretty much middle-aged clientele from the beginning and after a while I started losing a few every year, whether due to death, moving from the area, going broke, getting tired of playing, you name it. The volume of table players, especially high rollers, was dropping off, not to be replaced by a younger crowd. The increase in competition took a big toll out of the AC market, but I saw that things were starting to slip well before casinos became commonplace up and down the East Coast. The Atlantic City casinos thought prosperity would never end and thus never gave thought to continually redeveloping and replenishing the player base.

Getting back to Donald Trump: whenever he came down to the casino, I would meet with him and we would walk the entire property. He would make observations and ask questions. He didn't come down that often, but of course his presence was always known. One thing about Donald, he always wanted to know if I needed anything or what we needed to do make things better. He'd always ask if there was anything I thought he should do and I was always honest. If things weren't going well, I would tell him just that. I never got the same kind of feedback from the Harrah's people; they never seemed to want to know if things could be improved. Personally, I had to walk a tight rope between the partners: Donald had hired me, and my allegiance was to him, but officially I was working for Harrah's. It wasn't long before the tension was noticeable to all the employees. It worsened by the month and soon it was obvious to everyone that some kind of split was coming. The Trump people grew louder in expressing their unhappiness with Harrah's and the Harrah's people did not think the casino was making enough money. I always tried to stay neutral, but some Harrah's person might say to me, "I know you're Donald's guy." I really loved my job and did everything I could to keep a foot planted on both sides of the aisle. I must have been good at it. When the divorce finally came and Donald bought out Harrah's, the Harrah's executives all went over to the Marina site and as part of the agreement they were allowed to take 10 or 12 key people with them. I may have been viewed 'Donald's Guy,' but I was included in the group that was selected to move over to the Harrah's Marina.

When I was working at Trump and Donald called, I dropped whatever else I was doing. When Donald wanted me for something it was always for the benefit of the business. He might call and say that he was involved with some black tie affair in New York and wanted Rita and me to get dressed and get up there. We would take a limo to the airport and get a chopper ride to New York. Donald would provide me with a list of people who were going to be there and he might tell me that there were four or five people he wanted me to work on to get them down to the casino. He might point out someone and tell me he was a big hitter in Vegas. Rita and I would go over, say hello, and invite them down to play at our casino.

As much allegiance as I had to Donald, I was okay when the split came. The Harrah's people needed me and, with time, I found myself getting closer with them. They may not have had a native feel for the New Jersey market, but with their Vegas background they had excellent connections in sports and entertainment and they helped lure some big name entertainers and events to Convention Hall. To that point, I still don't think they had fully adapted to the Atlantic City market, but you could never say that everything they were doing was wrong.

I had my list of high rollers and knew they would follow me. As much as I liked Donald, I believed that Harrah's was probably the safer play for the long run, plus I also got a nice raise for making the switch. I told them I would be bringing my people over with me and that they had to be prepared to provide limos and choppers when needed. The first Harrah's guy I met with, an Executive Pres. named Ed Posey said, "Oh no, we don't do that." I told him you'd better start doing that, that's what high rollers have gotten accustomed to in Atlantic City.

I'll never forget the first guy I had to order a chopper for. One of my players from New York wanted to come down and he was used to being ferried back and forth by helicopter. Harrah's didn't want to do it, but I ordered the chopper anyway. My player comes down, loses about $200,000 and I get call at home from Posey that night asking if I have any more players like that. I said, "Yeah, I have about 2,000 more names that can afford a night like that." I was never questioned after that. I don't know that the Harrah's people ever fully got what Atlantic City was all about during my time there, but I did manage to get them to at least somewhat embrace the style that was required to do things the right way. They're still around and Donald is long gone from Atlantic City. Overall, the Harrah's gang was a good group of people. No one on their payroll was on the hustle, and I never felt like I had to watch my back because someone was trying to trip me up, make me look bad, or maybe try and lure one of my players. I can't say that Trump promoted a cutthroat organization, but it was definitely a more competitive environment. One thing I mastered there was to tell people as little as necessary about my business and where I could be found. If I were out of town, I would instruct the phone operators to simply answer, "He's out of the office." I didn't want anyone to know if I was say, in Virginia playing golf with a high roller. There was no need for anyone to know who I was talking to and I also didn't want to give anyone the opportunity to move in on one of my players because they found out I was away.

It was at Harrah's at Trump Plaza that I personally experienced a little of the celebrity treatment. I was doing well producing players who were dropping enormous sums on the gaming floor. As a reward, and also to provide events that would bring my high rollers in, I was feted with Joe Pagliei Celebrity Roasts and Joe Pagliei Invitational Golf Tournaments.

The first Pagliei Roast was an experience. I was given a budget of $10,000 to line up a rostrum of celebrity roasters. I asked Tom Brookshier, who had been a teammate with the Eagles and went on to become a nationally famous broadcaster doing NFL games on CBS. I offered Brookie $3,500, and he said, "That sounds good, but what the hell am I supposed to say about you. You barely played." I said "Why don't you open with something to the effect of 'I was offered 3500 good reasons to be here tonight to honor Joe Pagliei.'"

The marketing people wanted to come up with something special in the way of an invitation and suggested I ask LeRoy Neiman to design it. I told them, "I already did. LeRoy is doing the invitation." I went up to New York and met Leroy at his studio. I was looking out the window and LeRoy said, "Just stand there, don't move." I stood there for about 20 minutes and he said, "That's it." He did a Neiman portrait of me which became the cover design for the invitation and I still have original hanging my house. I didn't do a bad job in filling out the dais, getting some Hall of Fame talent coming in to roast me, including Tommy Lasorda, Julius Erving, Ray Nitschke and Billy Cunningham. We brought in a lot of money for the casino that night. I had no trouble attracting my high rollers with that lineup. The general public might not have recognized my name in the company of that crowd, but my high rollers and their families knew who I was. I always knew how to take care of them and made sure to never forget the wives.

It wasn't just the high rollers that followed me to Harrah's. I became great friends with most of the celebrities at each stop. I had met Joe Dimaggio at Bally's and he came over to Harrah's anytime I needed him. He was getting something like a minimum $25,000 appearance fee at the time and he told me, "Joe, if you ever need me, I'll do it for $8,500; and don't tell anyone, but if you really need me, I'll do it for nothing."

Most of the celebrities we brought in were great with the high rollers; others took some prodding to warm up. One night I brought Lynda Carter in to mingle with the them. I had paid her about $7,500 for a few hours of work. I brought her around to meet some of my players and get their pictures with her. She pulls me aside and complains, "Enough Joe, you're overexposing me." I replied, "For $7,500 I'm gonna expose you some more." She warmed up after that.

We'd set small events up for some of our best players. If I knew one of my important rollers had a birthday coming up, I might arrange a party for about 10 people with a sports celebrity or entertainer stopping by.

Donald was always aware when we had a major event going on but, other than meeting the celebrities and posing for pictures, he didn't really try to draw attention to himself. We took advantage of our physical link to Convention Hall to align ourselves with many of the events going on there and made sure our high rollers got the best seats. When the show was over they could walk over to our floor and start gambling. We got involved with everything: the Miss America Pageant, boxing matches, entertainment, and things like the 'Battle of the Sexes' tennis match with Martina Navartilova and Pam Shriver against Bobby Riggs and Vitas Gerulaitis. My biggest memory of that one was Bobby hustling one of my high rollers for about $10,000 on the golf course. I wasn't happy that he did that to one of my players, but when I confronted him, all he said was, "If you have any more like that I'll give you a cut of the action."

One night Neil Diamond was playing and I made arrangements for LeRoy Neiman to do some original sketches that we would use as high roller gifts. I get LeRoy situated off to the side on the stage and Diamond's manager comes over screaming that he was offsetting the balance of the stage and had to get off. I tell him that LeRoy's not going anywhere and then Neil Diamond comes over and tells the manager that, "It's okay, let him stay." There's no such thing as an ordinary night in the casino business.

Working for Donald Trump also brought excitement outside of the casino. It was during my time working for him that he bought the New Jersey Generals of World Football League. Owning a professional sports team in the New York market only served to raise Donald's public profile. He was about as publicity shy as George Steinbrenner. Even then Donald understood the value of branding and by keeping his name in the headlines he also, by extension, increased the visibility of Harrah's at Trump Plaza. In owning the Generals, Donald inherited possession of maybe the biggest name in football at the time, running back Herschel Walker. Herschel had won the Heisman Trophy playing for the University of Georgia, and he made a move that was unheard of for that era: he left school after his junior year to accept a three-year contract for the then huge sum of $5 million. Donald figured that it would be good for the casino to have Herschel come around once in a while and mingle with the high rollers.

Donald was hosting an event for Herschel up at the Meadowlands Stadium. He knew I was a football guy and thought it would be good for me to get to know Herschel. He invited Rita and me up to the function and sent a limo and helicopter for us. Rita always hate riding in choppers, but we left Atlantic City, stopped in New York for another event, then went over to the stadium in New Jersey. We arrived at Herschel's party and I went over to introduce myself and told him, "I'm Joe Pagliei. I don't know you, but I don't like you." That stunned him and he gave me a 'what-the-hell' look. It was tough for anybody to dislike Herschel Walker at that particular point in time. I told him, "I went to Clemson." Herschel understood and got a nice laugh out of it.

The Generals were representative of how Donald conducted all of his businesses. He tried to surround himself with big name stars and, at least initially, brought in smart, seasoned executives. While he picked their brains, he didn't necessarily do everything they advised, and eventually he thought he knew more than they did and proceeded to do things his own way. Within a few years many would come to blame Donald for the demise of the WFL when he pushed the league to move its schedule from spring to fall and initiated a lawsuit against the NFL. He was hoping to either cause a merger between the two leagues or win a hefty settlement. Neither occurred and the league folded.

I'm not saying that I was a Herschel Walker-magnitude star, but I did produce for Donald. He recognized my contributions to the bottom line of his casino and he did pay me well, though nowhere near the $5 million that Herschel was getting. I have to say that Donald Trump was always good to me and did treat me golden. At one point I had some tuition payments for my kids coming up and had been performing well, making money for the casino. I thought a bonus along the lines of $10,000 was not uncalled for. I went in to see Donald and laid out my case. He said to me, "I don't know Joe, the casino really isn't doing that well." I told him "Bullshit, don't tell me that," and proceeded to read from a paper that listed how much my best players had dropped at the casino in recent weeks. He said, "Alright, alright; you can pick up the money on Monday." He was a sharp, sharp businessman who didn't give away anything, but if you earned your money he took care of you.

Donald may not have given anything away, but in his heart he recognized that sometimes you had to spend money to get the biggest return. I think that was his biggest source of difference with the Harrah's people. They were content to run an operation devoid of any ostentation and get a steady return. Donald wanted to offer the best of everything and, in turn, get paid accordingly. In the end, they couldn't get together and Donald ended up with the whole casino to himself.

Do I believe that it was Donald's intent all along to wrest sole control of the casino?

I have no evidence, and he never confided that intention to me. The more he grasped the business, the more he would complain. He might say something along the lines, "I'm not impressed with so-and-so of Harrah's." In looking back, I guess he was building a case for divorce. He never understood the casino business as well as he liked to believe, but within the first year he had convinced himself that he could do a better job and bring in more money operating it on his own.

A typical day for me started about 10 am. First thing, I would review the VIP list, go over who was already here and who was coming in. I wanted to know what time they were arriving and, if they were my people or were sent by Donald, I would greet them. If they didn't have a host assigned to them, I would be there to say hello. I got to know the limo drivers and would instruct them to call me when they were 10 minutes away. You had to be aggressive if you wanted to be a successful host, nobody assigned the high rollers. It wasn't like a real estate office where a call might come in and the operator would point and say, "Joe, it's your turn." We had about a dozen hosts at both Bally's and Harrah's, and I would say that most of them never grasped the competiveness of the business. I enjoyed working a room, showing up where I might not know anybody and getting around, introducing myself. Going back to Clairton, I understood how the mind of a gambler worked. I was always a natural as a storyteller, and it was while working as a host that my routine became polished and I developed an easy rapport with the well-to-do crowd.

There was always so much money around. There was really no cap on expenses when it came to entertaining our best players. If one of my players mentioned to me that he wanted to come down, but his wife was holding him back, with a "What am I going to do there," I would arrange for an afternoon at the spa for her or a nice dinner at The Knife and Fork or another high-end restaurant.

Once, Donald asked me to entertain his brother Robert and his wife Blaine. Rita and I took them out to dinner along with front-of-the-house tickets to see Pavarotti at, I believe, Resorts. We became pretty good friends with Robert and Blaine. In most ways, Robert could not have been more different than Donald: always in the shadows, did nothing to attract attention; Blaine was much more outgoing. I know they eventually divorced in 2008.

If you want to talk about 'Main Attractions,' that is a role that Ivana Trump was born for. I spent a lot of time with the then Mrs. Trump whenever she was in town, Donald would ask me to stay by her side. She did all the talking, but I could never understand her. She could talk for an hour with her big accent and I'd just nod my head and smile, not knowing what I was agreeing with. She was very demanding and when she was in the house everyone tried to stay out of her way. She thought she knew everything and that even what she didn't know, she knew. The 'Boss's Wife' was a mild description to explain her behavior. The interaction between Donald and Ivana became noticeably less and less as the months wore on. Personal contact was virtually non-existent when Donald's 'lady friend,' Marla Maples, was onsite. Things were visibly tense and no one came out of their office when both Ivana and Marla were under the same roof. Marla had a suite that was connected to Donald's. One night I had a big player decide to stay overnight and we were out of suites. I had to make the executive decision to put him in Marla's unoccupied room. I carefully explained it to Donald the next day and he said, "That's okay; how much did the guy lose?" Donald was always looking to make a dollar wherever he could. Once he bought a yacht from, I believe, a Japanese businessman. I remember thinking, 'what does he need this boat for.' A few days later, he sold it for a 25% profit.

> *While working at Trump, one of Joe Pagliei Jr's. duties was to serve as an escort for Marla Maples:*
>
> *"When Marla Maples came down to the casino, one of my jobs was to take her to the back of the house and sneak her up to service elevators to her suite. Donald didn't want anyone to know she was onsite, especially Ivana. That was always a nervous time when Marla was in town."*

Tom Matte, Tommy Lasorda, Joe Pagliei holding Nitschke jersey and comedian Rich Little

To my knowledge, Trump was the first casino to give out complimentary tokens for use in the slots. In those days people were still pouring coins into the machines and the slot hosts would walk the floor giving the tokens out to players.

Rita and I did vote for Donald for President. I never saw that coming from that first day I met the young real estate guy at the restaurant in Bally's. He was good to me and my family, and I am proud to say that I worked closely with the President.

Joe Pagliei honoring Donald Trump

Bob Pellegrini, Tommy McDonald, Ed Khayat,
Pete Retzlaff, Joe Pagliei and Sonny Jurgensen

2nd from left Lou Rawls & 4th from left Sammy Davis Jr

Joe with Johnny Unitas, Rita (Joe's beautiful wife) and Willie Mosconi

Seated, l to r: Victoria Pagliei-Scott, Albert Pagliei Sr., Elizabeth Pagliei. Standing: Son-in-law Jimmy Scott, Lizanne Pagliei, Joe Pagliei Sr., Joe Pagliei Jr. and Patti Pagliei

Celebrity Billy Cunningham, 76er's (center back) holding on to Coach Chuck Daly, Al DoMenico, 76er's; Tom Brookshire, Eagles & Coach Fred Bruney, Eagles

9 – GOLF

A piece of advice; if you have the time to devote to becoming a decent golfer, do it. A number of good things fell into place for me in life and these opportunities were only enhanced by my ability to hold my own on a golf course.

As discussed previously, my first day on the job at Bally's, the fact that I was able to answer the question, "Hey Joe, can you play golf?" in the affirmative earned me the ongoing assignment of serving as the travelling golf companion to Willie Mays. To this day, golf continues to open so many opportunities for me. At 83 years old, I'm shooting my age, still play in about a dozen invitational outings a year, and enjoying weekly rounds with my golfing buddies. These past few years, I look around at these outings and realize that I'm usually the oldest golfer on the course. Each year I see fewer and fewer of my contemporaries at these events. I used to play in about twice as many events and I suspect that my age is the reason I'm getting fewer invites. Mistake on their part, I still work out every day and part of my routine at the gym includes exercises to help keep me limber when it comes to swinging a golf club. I can still hit a long ball AND keep it in play.

Terese Brittingham, one of the organizers of the annual Keller Williams + Mutual of Omaha Golf Outing for Alex's Lemonade Stand Foundation held annually in Phoenixville, PA, bridges two of Joe Pagliei's passions- golf and horseracing. Terese and her husband were part of the group that purchased an ugly duckling horse, named Afleet Alex, that no one else wanted at auction, and cheered as that horse won both the Preakness and Belmont Stakes in 2005. Joe has been a regular supporter of the Alex's golf outing and has become close friends with the Brittinghams through these outings.

"Joe is the nicest man I've ever met. I met him at a Maxwell Football Banquet and we talked about horse racing and our golf outing. Joe started coming to our outing and has been wonderful. He's recruited a lot of people and brought out local celebrities like the newsmen Tom Lemaine and Bill Baldini. Tommy McDonald used to come every year with Joe and between the two of them, they made everyone laugh. Tommy and Joe were the life of the party.

"I can understand why so many celebrities always wanted to be friends with Joe- it's because Joe genuinely likes you. Influential people are comfortable with him because he is not a fake. He has the rare combination of having a magnetic personality, but at the same time he is like a loving grandfather. People love talking to him.

"Both Joe and I like meeting people and he's helped us so much with bringing people together for a great cause. He always has a standing foursome at our golf events."

I'm one of the many natives of Western Pennsylvania who, in the 1950's, were inspired by Arnold Palmer to pick up a golf club for the first time. Arnie, the kid from Latrobe with working class roots, was responsible for igniting a golf craze in an area otherwise dotted with factories and industrial plants. I couldn't escape the influence of Arnold Palmer, even when I was living in Philadelphia. My roommate there, Billy Ray Barnes, was a graduate of Wake Forest which is also where Arnie had attended college and was the star of the golf team. Billy Ray told me that Arnie was also responsible for getting a lot of people in Demon Deacon country to pick up a golf club for the first time. Billy Ray was my first steady golfing partner. Tom Brookshier would also join us on occasion. We didn't know what we were doing, but we had a hell of a good time.

Truth was, when I was growing up we really didn't think of golf as a manly game, but Arnold Palmer helped change that perception more than anyone. This big, strong, good-looking guy from coal country, who played with such a swagger, made us all want to give golf a try.

For all of the influence that Arnie had on me, he is one of the few major sports celebrities of the past 60 years that I never met. I don't know how he eluded me. We came close once when I invited him to an outing at Bally's. I negotiated with his business manager and thought I could make a deal, but their side was stuck on a $30,000 appearance fee, plus expenses, for Arnie to fly into New Jersey in his personal plane. I had a lot of leeway with my bosses at the casino, but Arnie's price tag was a little too steep for them to swallow.

While I may have missed out on meeting Arnie, I did spend time with other golfing royalty, including Jack Nicklaus and Gary Player. One of my good golfing friends is Judy Clark, who was married to the late professional golfer, Gardner Dickinson. I was at Loxahatchee Golf Club in Florida and Judy had arranged for me to have a 9 am lesson with Gardner. I showed up and, at about 10 minutes to 9, I get a call that Gardner can't make it because 'Jack is coming down.' I'm asking, "Jack, who?" Of course it was Jack Nicklaus. The Golden Bear comes walking down the steps, I introduced myself and mentioned that we had a friend in common, Tom Matte, who played for the Baltimore Colts and was a classmate of his at Ohio State. Jack was a great guy and really got interested when he learned that I knew Matte, who was a terrific golfer, a scratch player, in his own right. All Jack wanted to talk about was football. He was impressed that I had played football even though he was probably bigger than me.

Jack loved hearing my Tom Matte stories. I told him that whenever we had a Joe Pagliei Roast in Atlantic City there would be an accompanying Pagliei golf tournament, and if Tom Matte was able to attend, I would assign him to my team. Of all the celebrities that I've played with over the years, Matte was hands down the best golfer. With Matte as a teammate, I won one of my namesake tournaments. This raised some eyebrows and I never stacked the team in my own tournament after that. That year when they were announcing the winning team, someone complained that I shouldn't be able to win my own tournament. My bosses decided to let the victory stand and the prize for each member of the winning team was a Gucci watch. After that I decided that it might be better that I don't win my own outing. I made sure I teamed my high rollers with the best-playing celebrities. In truth, not many of the celebrities were that good, but I'd estimate that 95% of my high rollers were also bad-to-average golfers.

Getting back to The Golden Bear, he and I were having such a good time talking Tom Matte and football that he invited me back into the clubhouse and we continued the conversation for about 15 or 20 minutes. He told me that if I ever came back down to Jupiter or Tequesta that he was going to be angry if I didn't call him. He said that he would get me on any golf course in Florida.

Over the years people have asked me why I didn't talk golf with Jack Nicklaus when I had the opportunity. One of the things that I learned over the years is that one of the secrets of golf is that anyone who knows what they are doing keeps it a secret. They don't want you to know what they know, unless you're willing to part with a lot of money. A teaching pro like Butch Harmon will get you straightened out if you're willing to part with a mortgage payment or two in exchange for a lesson.

I also became friends with Gary Player and even closer with his son Marc. I met Gary through my late brother-in-law and close friend, Manny Occhipinti. Manny was member of Jasna Palona Golf Club near Princeton, New Jersey and Gary was making an appearance there. Manny was a great guy, married to Rita's sister Dolores. He passed away much too young, but left a great family behind in sons, Jimmy and John, and daughters, Julie and Jill.

I started playing golf right after college. I was back in Clairton the summer after my senior year and a local pro, George Philips was brave enough to begin teaching me the game. George was connected with Oakmont, the legendary golf club where they have played nine US Opens and three PGA Championships. It was at Oakmont, not some local public course, where I played my first round of golf. I didn't even own a set of clubs but George hooked me up and took me over to Oakmont. Here I am at a nationally-renowned course and my golf career could not have gotten off to a more disastrous start. First hole, I set up in the tee box and the club flies out of my hands and lands on the roof of the clubhouse. George had to get a ladder and climb up to retrieve my club. A buddy of mine who was joining us was running late. When he got to the club he asked the pro if Joe Pagliei was on the course and the response was, "I don't know Joe Pagliei, but some crazy bastard just threw his club up on the roof."

Rough initiation aside, I continued to play regularly that summer and showed some signs of being a decent golfer. For the first time, I saw a glimpse of the doors that could be opened through golf. My high school and college football careers earned me some recognition as a local celebrity and, as such, I started getting invited to various golf outings. Later in life, when I took my first casino job, the combination of a sports career and golf would begin to pay big-time dividends.

I could always drive the ball and over the years tried to become an all-around student of the game. I was always a good guy to have on your team in a scramble outing: I could hit anywhere from 250, up to about 320 yards when I got a good run out of the ball.

I had been playing for about five years and in 1964 my friend John Villari, the owner of the Mill Restaurant, offered to sponsor me at Riverton Country Club near my home in Pennsauken. He thought I would fit in well at the club, but he also cautioned me that there were only one or two Italian families that were members. A screening meeting was set up and Rita and I found ourselves sitting across from five male club members. This was not a nice, casual, let's-get-to-know-each-other interview. They really grilled us, asking all sorts of personal questions, things like what places we liked to go to and who our friends were. I was getting really upset and told them that for the money they were looking for to join this club, I should be the one asking questions. I'm thinking what the hell am I getting myself into and questioning if I really want to do this. I went over to visit John in his restaurant and told him he could keep his club. I let him know that I started asking them questions and he said "Shit Joe, why did you that, now you probably won't get in." A few days later I got a call from one of my interviewers informing me that we were in. I stayed there as a member and Rita and I had a great time. The only reason I left was because Bally's gave me a membership at Atlantic City County Club in 1979 so that I could entertain our high rollers there.

One of my first big wins as part of a golf foursome was the NFL Alumni Tournament at Whitemarsh Country Club in suburban Philadelphia. I brought a group up from Bally's and, by winning, we earned the right to represent Philadelphia at the Alumni's national tournament at Torrey Pines in California. It was called The Super Bowl of Golf, with good players from all around the country. We finished eighth or ninth and were pleased with our showing.

Bally's, Harrah's, Trump; I was the travelling golf ambassador at each of the casinos where I worked. Donald Trump would send me all over the country for golf outings. While I never did get to play with Donald, I did see him hit the ball. He had a good swing and word around the casino was that he was decent golfer.

Golf was very important when you were around Donald Trump. He sent me to some of the nation's most exclusive clubs to play in various outings. I might show up for work and he'd tell me get your clubs, you're going down to Alabama to play with the Governor; or you're going to Florida to play with the Attorney General. Everywhere I went, I was expected to invite people back to the casino. It seemed that many, if not most, of the big time casino players also played golf. In addition to playing with them in the different outings, many of them would also invite me to play at their private clubs. Casinos and golf go together. I learned that if you represented a casino and were a decent enough player, you were invited for more rounds of golf than you could ever possibly accept. I played to about a 16-18 handicap in those days. I was a popular pick for scramble teams because I could really drive the ball. My putting wasn't bad either and it seemed that at least once a round I could be counted on to sink a long one. I also learned the importance of 'tanking' or taking it easy when I was on the course with high rollers. I tried to keep it close and, when prudent, would even let them beat me. I wanted them leaving the course in an upbeat frame of mind if they were going to be gambling that night.

My favorite celebrity teammate was Joe DiMaggio. He and I first played together on a team at the Italian Open. I was really fit at the time and Joe was about 20 years older than me. I would outdrive him on nearly every hole and he'd look at me and say, "I used to hit the ball like that." He was getting up in years, but Joe could still hit the ball well. His golf swing was almost as pretty as his baseball swing. Joe and Tommy Lasorda became key figures, almost like my golfing godfathers. Whenever they played in an outing they would recommend that the host also invite me. If it was a charity event, I'd usually bring along a generous donation check from the casino. If I invited Tommy to one of my casino outings, I could always count on him to also make a few phone calls and bring in some other big name athletes.

Joe Pagliei Jr. recalls a trip to Florida with his parents where his dad was playing in an outing at the invitation of Joe DiMaggio:
"My wife and I were sharing a suite with my parents at a resort. One morning there's a knock at the door and I can't believe Joe DiMaggio is standing there. He said that he forgot his razor and asked if we had a spare that he could borrow. I went into the bathroom and dug out a cheap disposable razor and gave it to him. I still tell the story; I can't believe that I gave a razor to Joe DiMaggio. I should have asked for it back and kept it as a souvenir."

Joe and I had remained friends since I rescued him from a horde of reporters during my early days at Bally's. He was a man who was true to his word. Out of gratitude that day, he told me that at any time, he would do whatever he could to help me and he always came through. If he was available, he always came to my casino events and you knew that if you announced that Joe DiMaggio would be in attendance, everyone would show up. If I had slots for 72 golfers every one of them would be filled. I'd tell Joe that I promised each one of them a signed baseball, and he'd groan and say "Oh, come on!" But I'd send out for 72 baseballs and he'd sign each one. We had to have an assembly line going, one guy took the balls out of the box, another did the unwrapping and handed it to Joe, a third person would re-wrap the signed ball and put in back in the box. On Sunday mornings he and I would go to an early mass together. Because of Joe, I could never be friendly with Ted Williams. Joe wanted to be recognized as 'The Greatest Living Baseball Player,' and was never comfortable if Ted was around. If I mentioned that I was thinking of inviting Ted down for a banquet, Joe would say, "I don't think that we need him." Joe's opposition probably didn't matter because I also heard that Ted didn't care to attend any functions where Joe would be present, so in all likelihood he wouldn't have shown up any way.

I also learned that there were two names that were absolutely never to be brought up in the presence of Joe: one was Marilyn Monroe, the other was Frank Sinatra. For obvious reasons Joe never wanted to discuss Marilyn, and he carried a bitter grudge against Sinatra for some very uncomplimentary and outright crude remarks that Frank had made about Marilyn until his death.

Joe and I became great friends. He would call me at home and say that he was coming into town and ask if I could put him up at the casino. I'd say, "Are you kidding, how about a suite?" Joe's appearance fee at the time was a minimum $25,000, but after we became friends, he told me, "Joe, I like you and because you're Italian, I'll show up for you for $8,500…but don't ever tell anyone about our deal." In one of the greatest displays of friendship that I've ever experienced Joe also told me that if I ever needed a job, or if I really needed him, he would make an appearance for nothing, zero dollars. If I asked Joe to go into the dining room and say hello to one of my players who had a rough night at the tables, he'd do so without hesitation. I'd bring a photographer along and the player would go home happy with a photo of himself and Joe Dimaggio.

Joe told me that his loyalty was to me, not the casino I was working at, and promised to follow me wherever I was working. Joe used to bring Rita and me up to New York for the big Welcome Home Yankees banquet at the start of every baseball season. Joe was always protected by security at these type functions, but as soon as he saw us he would wave Rita and me over and make sure we got the same treatment and privileges that he did. We had each other's phone numbers and he'd call the house, Rita would answer and she'd hear, "Hi Rita, it's Joe Dimaggio, is Joe around." When a new condominium development, Boca Teeca, was built in Boca Raton, Joe was given a free unit in exchange for the use of his name. He invited us down to stay with him and play golf. Joe also invited us to Chicago for an Italian American Sports Hall of Fame Banquet. We went out there with Joe, Tommy Lasorda, Willie Mosconi, Joey Giardello and Ed Liberatore, who was a scout for the Phillies. We were all on the same flight and Rita turns to me and says, "Joe, God forbid this plane goes down; there goes the Italian American Sports Hall of Fame!" At that banquet, when all of the celebrities were introduced, the emcee mentioned that I had played for the Philadelphia Eagles and the New York Titans. With all of the really big names that were in the audience this news made little impact with the crowd, most people were going to the big name tables for autographs. Tommy McDonald got up to the mic and said something like I was also a two-time All American, a two-time All Conference, then added that I also had a $15,000 donation check from Bally's; that brought a lot more people to our table.

Joe arranged for me to get an invite to the Yogi Berra Golf Classic at Montclair Country Club in North Jersey. All of the great old Yankees players used to show up for this outing and this helped open up all sorts of Yankee connections for me. The first time I went up to the outing, I brought Yogi a nice sweater from Bally's. He liked it so much he asked if I could send another one for his wife, which I of course did as soon as I got back to the casino. We had Billy Martin come down to the casino and Al Rosen brought him over to say hello to me. From there, Billy heads over to the gaming area and within a half hour we get a call that a guy is starting trouble on the floor. Yogi and Billy were both Yankees, and Billy Martin was notorious for getting in brawls. I went down with security and we talked Billy out of getting into a fight. He calmed down and was civil after that.

George Steinbrenner, the Yankees owner, came down to the casino a short time after the 1981 World Series was completed. The Yankees had lost to the Dodgers in six games and, as was well-reported at the time, Steinbrenner was carrying his arm in a sling. It was all over the news: he had claimed that he got into an elevator fight with a couple of drunken Dodgers' fans who had made disparaging remarks about the Yankees and New York. Steinbrenner always stuck to the story that he was defending the honor of New York, but the two brawlers were never located or identified and the inside story was The Boss broke his hand punching the elevator wall in frustration. George was great when he was down at the casino, I asked him about the fight and he told me a hybrid of the two stories; that he broke his hand when he took a swing at one of the guys who was busting his balls, missed, and hit the elevator wall. He invited me up to see a Yankees game in his private suite. I brought along a buddy of mine who was a big Yankees fan. We met Steinbrenner at his stadium office to watch the game from the suite that extended out from the office. We step in the box and there's a guy sitting in one of the seats, he looks at us and says, "Hey, George." Steinbrenner walked over to his phone, called security and told them that there was someone sitting in his seats and to get up there and get him the hell out. I also got to go up to the broadcast booth and meet Phil Rizzuto.

I'm still in awe of the opportunities that were created for me through golf.

One summer Rita and I were on our way to Saratoga for the horse races and we stopped on Long Island for an outing at Bethpage Black Golf Course. A friend of mine, Jack Paltani, had organized the outing. Jack was a scratch golfer and a member at Grande Oaks Golf Club in Florida where the movie *Caddyshack* was filmed. Jim Nantz was one of the celebrity guests and I got to spend some time with him. He was a genuinely good guy and enjoyed hearing the stories of my Clemson days.

As mentioned previously, of all the professional athletes I played with, the best golfer was Tom Matte. He supposedly held his own on the course with Jack Nicklaus when they were classmates at Ohio State. No doubt he also picked up a lot of free lessons playing with Jack. Among the other good golfers I played with were Ron Jaworski, Joe Pisarcik and Dan Marino. Lenny Moore and Bobby Mitchel were both very intense and competitive players as well.

Lawrence Taylor was about a 3 or 4 handicap. I played at his outing in Williamsburg, Virginia one year and invited him up to my outing in Atlantic City. Getting the most popular Giants player to come up New Jersey would make a big impact on many of my high rollers. Lawrence agreed to make an appearance, but a few days after the LT outing I was sitting in my office at the casino and my phone rings. The caller identifies himself as Lawrence Taylor's agent and he tells me that LT is not going to be able to make it. I said, "What are you talking about? Lawrence promised he'd play." The agent tells me that everything has to go through him and he's not going to okay it. I hang up the phone and call Lawrence directly, tell him about the agent and he replies, "Joe, I promised you I will be there and I WILL be there." I told him that I would send a chopper for him. The agent calls me back the next day, I told him I'd get right back to him, put him on hold and left him talking into dead air. The guy could still be holding on to his phone for all I cared, I never went back to that call. The guy was jacking me around and I dumped him. Lawrence comes up to the casino and he is great with everyone. One of my high rollers is having dinner and when he finds out that LT is in the house, he sends a message to me: He'll donate $10,000 to Julius Erving's Lupus charity if he could get a picture with Taylor. I told the guy not to move and ran down to the gaming floor to get Lawrence. He's playing Craps and tells me, "Not now, Joe." I told him about the $10,000 donation and he ran upstairs with me, took the picture, signed some autographs and ran back down to the gaming floor. The high roller gave me the check on the spot. Lawrence Taylor was always great with everyone anytime I had him at a casino. I was at Grand Oaks Country Club in Fort Lauderdale and watched Taylor play Michael Jordan in a head to head match. I remember the first hole, which was about 400 yards and Taylor took out a 2 iron and put the ball within 90 feet of the pin. I don't recall who won, but I'm sure some big money changed hands.

Willie Mays was a pretty good golfer and I was in awe during those early days at Bally's when I was running around as the Say Hey Kid's personal golfing companion. I'd show up for work and be told, not asked, "You're playing golf in New York on Wednesday with Willie. Be ready, the limo will pick you up early." I loved it: golf, high rollers and Willie Mays. What was there not to like. Willie was a 10-12 handicap, but a peculiar thing about him, he was one of the few people who would give out a lower handicap number. We all know golfers who add a few strokes to their handicap to gain a better advantage, but Willie would tell people he was 5. I never asked him about it, maybe it was ego, maybe he wanted to make it more of a challenge. Every outing we went to Willie would stay close to me; he wasn't comfortable with crowds. He'd say, "Come on Joe, let's you and me go over there where it's quiet." Things never seemed to stay quiet long as the crowd would always gravitate to Willie. Our contract with Willie called for him to give us three days a month, but if I needed him for an extra day or two he usually agreed.

Not all golfers played strictly by the rules. I won an outing with Jim Taylor as a partner. We were playing in best ball scramble and Jim was a pretty good golfer, but If he didn't like any of the shots, he'd say, "Let's play so we can have some fun," and he'd move his ball over to where we could get a better shot. A guy like Chuck Bednarik, he wouldn't let you move a ball an inch if you were stuck behind a tree, "You hit it there, you play it out of there." One year I won the longest drive competition at an outing at Whitemarsh Country Club, which was Chuck's home club. He said to me, "What kind of juiced up ball are you hitting, you must have hit a sprinkler head and got a lucky bounce." I could always hit the ball. I'm especially deadly these days now that I'm hitting off the seniors tee. I'm 83 and I'm putting the ball out past guys a lot younger than me.

Whenever I'm assigned as the celebrity in a foursome, first thing I do is check out the other players' clubs and then look for a sun tan. If a guy is pasty white in August, I know he isn't much of a golfer. If a guy has something like Kmart or some no-name brand club in his bag, I know he isn't a serious player. You may end up with partners who have nice tans and expensive clubs, but after a hole or two, you knew whether or not you're going to be in on the action that day. When guys are celebrating for getting pars, you're not taking home any prizes that day. I want birdies when we're playing best ball. If you do come to the realization that you aren't going to win anything, you might start moving the ball around a little bit and let the group enjoy themselves. These guys may have pooled their money together or someone's company wrote out a check to enter, so you may as well let them have some fun.

I was always amazed at the impact of having your name associated with a golf tournament. I had just a so-so career as a professional athlete, but was later privileged to be part of five Joe Pagliei Classics when I was working at the casinos. Not many people remembered me as a football player, but I could be in upstate New York, South Carolina or Florida, and someone would hear my name and say, "Oh, yeah, I played in your outing in Atlantic City."

It was such an honor the first time the Bally's people approached me and said, "Hey Joe, why don't you host a golf outing for the high rollers." The first phone call I made was to Tommy Lasorda. We had first met at the Bally's Sports Legends Banquet. Tommy was there with his wife Jo and, since he was from Norristown, this was a homecoming for him. Tommy helped elevate me from the basement to the top floor when I was starting out as a casino host. He knew everybody and, whenever I needed a big name appearance, he'd go into his address book and deliver a celebrity for me. Everybody loved Tommy and he was a great friend. For the outing, Tommy gave me a list of celebrity names and numbers, told me who to call, and said that if they didn't respond or declined the invitation just let him know. Nobody was stronger than Tommy Lasorda when it came to rounding up celebrities. For me, Tommy delivered people like Joe Torre, Eric Gregg and Bill Cosby. He wanted to bring in Bob Costas to serve as master-of-ceremonies, but I had to turn him down on that one as I had already committed to my old friend Harry Kalas, the great Philadelphia Phillies announcer.

I know Bill Cosby is toxic these days, but back then he was at the height of his popularity and was great when I needed him. At one roast, he told me that he would be standing in back of room with a cigar in his mouth when I was doing introductions. He said to have a spotlight shined on him when he lit the cigar and he would then start roasting Lasorda. The year we roasted him, I got a call from Joe Torre telling me that he had heard about the Lasorda roast and wanted to know why he wasn't invited. I told him that I didn't have his contact info, but would be happy to fly him down for the event.

Tommy Lasorda opened so many doors, even almost getting me in to meet Frank Sinatra. Frank was playing at Resorts and Tommy and I went over to see the show. Afterward we wanted to go backstage to say hello. Tommy got in, I didn't, but they brought me back a personalized autographed picture. Everyone knew Tommy Lasorda, even the Chairman of the Board.

My high roller invitation list for the golf outings started with guys who had credit lines of $35,000 and up. In putting together the groups, I would start by pairing the best celebrity golfer with the worst high roller. I would then put the best high roller golfer with the worst celebrity, and continue to build the groups from there. My goal was that by the time I got to the middle groupings I would have a 15 handicap celebrity playing with a 15 handicap high roller. I tried to balance things so that everyone could feel that they had a shot. I was always able to get big money people to come down to my casino-sponsored outings, who could turn down an invitation to play golf with a Willie Mays or a Joe Dimaggio?

Some of the casino players that I invited by phone at first said that they couldn't make it, but then when they got the invitation in the mail that listed all of the celebrity guests, they'd change their mind, call back and said, "Joe, I'll be there." These events were very successful for the casino, one of my outings accounted for a $900,000 win for the house. The bean counters were always happy after my events. We'd get as many as 500 people at the banquet the night before the outing.

We invited Casey Stengel to one of my early outings at Bally's. Casey didn't play golf, but we figured he'd be great at the banquet. I had ordered Bally's golf bags as gifts for all of the golfing celebrities and when Casey found out, he wanted one, too, even though he didn't golf. I asked Billy Weinberger what to do and he said, "Just give him a damned bag."

The best professional golfer that I had the privilege to play with was Donna Caponi. Donna captained our Harrah's team to win the Shop Rite Classic at Seaview Country Club. I loaded the team that year; there was no way we could lose. My hand-picked Murderers Row included Billy Care: a scratch golfer and the best amateur player I ever saw. He once lost to Jack Nicklaus in the quarterfinals of the US Amateur and holds the course record, 62, at Atlantic City Country Club; Don Morano: a scratch golfer and all around hustler in the Al Besselink-mode; and John Olooney: a casino vice president; Donna and I completed the team. We won with authority. Donna has remained a close friend for many years, Rita and I both love her dearly.

Billy Care was and remains today a great amateur player. He's one of the best players I've ever seen on a golf course. At 16-, 17-years old he was breaking records at golf clubs around Atlantic City. He was also a great all-around hustler. One time he and another guy were playing in a match for about $4,000 a team. The money was put up and given to Billy to hold. He stopped at the racetrack on his way to golf course and blew all of the money on a sure thing. He was told that this horse couldn't lose and, of course, that horse ended up coming in dead last. When he got to the golf course he explained what happened and the attitude was 'that's Billy for you;' you couldn't stay mad at the guy. He was always trying to cut his friends in on his action and could have made it on the professional golf tour, he was that good. I never saw anyone better with a wedge in his hands, from 90 yards in he could put the ball within 10 inches of the cup. Another year I brought him to an NFL Alumni Tournament in South Jersey. I again stacked the team with Don Morano and Donna Caponi. We won going away. When one of the guys who was affiliated with the tournament saw the team I was putting in, he said, "There's no way you can lose."

Another one of my favorite golf buddy characters is Al Besselink, another hustler of legendary proportions. I first met him at Riverton Country Club in the late 1960's. He liked to talk football and we became friendly. He also liked to play golf and win a lot of money. He was always putting matches together by going up to guys and asking two questions, "How many strokes do you need and how much money do you have?"' If you asked Besse how much money he had, he would answer, "None, I don't lose."

I've had a great life on the golf course. Thank you to George Philips for all of your patience. If you had thrown me out of Oakmont the day my club flew onto the clubhouse roof, I might have never come back.

Joe Pagliei and famous top pro golfer, Gary Player

Ron Jaworoski and Joe Pagliei (right) at Yogi Berra's golf tournament.

Joe DiMaggio, my golf partner

10 – TODAY

I am 83 years old as I write this and my mind is sound enough that I have written most of this book from memory. I am blessed. Rita and I have our health, our energy, our family and each other. Six mornings a week I'm on the exercise machines at the local LA Fitness health club. At least two or three days a week, I go straight from the gym to Ramblewood Country Club in Mt. Laurel to hit some golf balls and work on my short game. Ramblewood is one of the many golf courses owned and operated by my friend Ron Jaworski. I give Jaws credit, he manages all of his courses like a family business. I guess it is a family business as his lovely wife Liz, son BJ and a bunch of other family members are all actively involved. I'll say this about Jaws, I've been playing the area golf courses for more than 50 years and every time Jaws takes one over, everybody on staff suddenly becomes friendlier, from the club pros to the starters to the bartenders. Ronnie does a great job and passes that same enthusiasm that you see on television down to his staff. I'm glad he operates a golf course that is close to my house.

This routine gets broken up on Sunday as Rita and I have our regular seats for the 10 am mass at St. John Neuman. From there we stop for the best breakfast in South Jersey at the White House Restaurant. Nobody does breakfast like Nick Patouhas and Paul Diaminatis and we get to see all of the other Sunday morning regulars who have become good friends through the years.

I've also just been inducted into the charter class for the new Clairton Sports Hall of Fame. Since I'm the oldest inductee, I was named Grand Marshall and earned the spot in the lead parade car. My old buddy Jim Kelly was also inducted. The high school stadium has been named after him, so the ceremonies took place in Jim Kelly Stadium.

It's a good thing that I'm able to get to the gym on a regular basis, as good food is still an important part of my life. I like to eat and working out helps offset that particular vice. Rita always tells people that one of the first things I asked her the night we met was "Do you know how to cook?" She was the cutest thing I ever saw, had the sweetest personality, and when she answered "Yes," I was beginning to believe that she just might be the complete package. That's a Clairton thing: first you look for a pretty girl and then you inquire about her kitchen skills. That was my criteria for finding a wife. It might sound a little primitive today, but it worked for us and we've had a beautiful marriage for 57 years now (and I get a great meal every night).

I like food. I don't mean to imply that I choose my friends solely on their culinary skills, but if a guy can cook, that makes him an even better pal. One of my close friends for more than 30 years is Bobby Chez, the famed crab cake impresario. A couple of times a month Rita and I pick up at one of his restaurants and it's a special treat to get invited to one of the parties that he and his wife Linda hold in their house. The menu starts with crab cakes and eggplant and ends with the most deadly dessert table ever established. Rita can usually be found hanging around the sweets. Their collie Bentley is classier than a lot of the guys I played ball with.

I still follow the ponies and, if a horse that I like is running, I'll go over to Parx Racetrack in Bensalem and bet a few bucks.

I still love being around the casinos as much as I do the racetrack, but you will never find me on the gaming floor. It's probably no coincidence that all of my friends who like to gamble also happen to be broke. If I learned anything in all of those years that I worked in the casinos, it's to keep your money in your pocket. I don't go down to Atlantic City that much anymore. It just doesn't have that Emerald City magic that remains stored in my memory. When I do visit I stay at Caesars Atlantic City. Joe Watson, a senior vice president over there, is one of the sharpest casino executives that I've ever been around and they run a good operation.

Living in Mt. Laurel, we're surrounded by good friends. Rita's been in the Philly area her whole life and I've been around since 1959. My buddy Ken Dunek, a former Eagle, is doing a great job publishing JerseyMan and PhillyMan magazines, and as a golfing buddy, man, can he hit the ball a long way. Brian Propp, a former Philadelphia Flyer, is another good friend. For years I used to win the longest drive competition in many of the golf outings that I played in. Brian figured out how to turn his hockey stroke into a golf swing and I stopped winning the longest drive in any of the outings that he was entered in.

There are so many people to acknowledge; I can write all day and still not say enough.

None of my success as a casino executive would have been possible without Joe Dimaggio, Tom Lasorda or Willie Mays. Bobby Shantz, the former New York Yankee and Philadelphia Athletic, has always been available for me. The late, great Phillies announcer Harry Kalas and Richie Ashburn were dear friends who could always be counted on. Coach Lou Holtz became a friend and always told me, "Joe, I wish I could have recruited you to punt for me at Notre Dame'.

My old coach Frank Howard, for bringing me to Clemson, and then telling Coach Wally Butts to send the 'dumb Italian kid' back from Georgia when I tried to defect. You gave me a great four years, Coach, and you were a crowd pleaser whenever I invited you up to Atlantic City.

The Clairton Boys: Nello Fiore, John 'Tiggy' Tenaglia, Arnold 'Spider' Ronandelli and Nunzio Chelli, who was a hell of a blocking guard on our high school team.

It pains Rita and me that our best friends, Tommy and Patty McDonald are struggling with separate health issues. Our prayers are always with them. Pete Ciarrocchi, the owner of Chickie and Pete's has been a great supporter of the Philadelphia Chapter of the NFL Alumni Group that I've been active with. He always provided me with a space in one of his restaurants when I need to hold a meeting.

My buddy Frank Kerbeck always came through when I was looking secure a luxury car for one of my high rollers. He's always had the best selection of eye popping cars on the east coast.

Merrill Reese, the legendary voice of the Eagles has been a good friend and frequent golf partner.

These days a shopping center sits on the site of Garden State Park, but I don't see Wegmans or Home Depot or any of the other stores when I'm stopped at a traffic light on Route 70. My memory takes over and I see people like Bobby Camac, Max Clark or Dennis Milton Heimer and other old friends who are no longer with us. I'm not the best at praying, but I always try to remember my friends, especially those who aren't around anymore.

For all of the good times, things weren't always easy. There were a few holes I had to dig out of and none of it would have been possible without Rita. She's been a constant plus through all of my dealings. She's always been there for all of us, including our children Vicki, Joe, Patti and Lizanne. The kids have given us six wonderful and intelligent grandchildren, Taylor and Brandon Scott; Victoria and Vanessa Pagliei; LuLu Simpson and Ava Grace Hales.

Our daughters, Patti Simpson and Liz Hales, operate a very successful jewelry business, Waxing Poetic. Those two are tough; real competitors. Vicki's husband Jim Scott owns CW Clarke Used Cars in New Jersey; and Joe Jr. is a top executive with the Stronach Group, owners and operators of six of the nation's leading racetracks.

Me, I'm just a son of an Italian immigrant from Clairton who got the opportunity to get out of a dusty steel town because I scored a few touchdowns for Clairton High.

Thanks to the National Football League for the opportunity to serve the retired players for over 16 years. Holding the offices of President for four years, Vice President for four years and Treasurer for eight years to present day.

If I were making my own decisions at the time, I would have stayed behind as a Clairton Bad Boy and not taken advantage of the ticket out that football was offering. I had this girlfriend at the time, and even with 105 colleges vying for my services, I didn't want to leave town. I was ready to take a job at the steel mill and settle down. I had no interest in college. It was my good fortune that my father, who arrived in this country about 30 years earlier with no job or language skills, had the good sense to tell me, "You no go to-a college; you no-a my son."

Pop, thank you, and I'm glad I listened. I would have missed out on all of these memories if it weren't for you.

Joe Pagliei and Joe Namath
at Jets a golf tournament

11 – LESSONS LEARNED

I'll take a few minutes to talk about the process of making decisions that can have an effect on your entire life. Playing mind games on yourself can make all the difference in achieving success. You can't be prepared for everything that will pop up and confront you, but you have to equip yourself with the tools that will enable you to make the best decision when the time comes. This isn't easy because there will always be someone around who does not want to see you excel or, at the minimum, put yourself in a better position than they are in. You are not going to get ahead if you let these people influence you.

Sometimes you have to have the presence of mind to make the choice that goes against what certain people are whispering in your ear. You have to pick and choose and carefully sort your way through a maze of advice. You have to put serious thought into making the right choices, otherwise you will end up on the losing side.

I've been fortunate to have certain friends that genuinely wanted me to do well and come out ahead of whatever the forces were that were trying to beat me down. For all of those good friends, I've had as many jealous people involved in my life who would always degrade my skills and capabilities. Don't let these people take you down with them. Know who your true friends are, if you have three of them in your life, you are blessed.

Maybe I didn't have the career in professional football that I wanted, but I did make it and I'm damned proud of that. I'm among the tiny percentage of football players who got to buckle the chin strap for a paycheck and I did that in three professional leagues.

The people who want to minimize your successes are around at all stages of life. They are always going to try and infuse you with enough doubt to weaken your ability to make sound decisions. Many of them have hit their ceilings in life and they don't want to see you rising above them. It truly bothers them to see you get more credit or recognition than, in their minds, you deserve. This is especially true if it exceeds the attention that they are getting.

One of the toughest things in life is fighting off the negativity that others are trying to introduce into your life. These are people who try to quietly steer you away from clearheaded thinking. You are not always going to be right, but make the decision that fits your personality and beliefs. If you do that, and are willing to put in the work to support your decision, in most cases you will reap the rewards.

Looking back, and using both my heart and my head, I was right about 90% of the time when I did the opposite of what someone who did not really have my best interests in mind was advising me to do. I learned that you have to be prepared to work and think a little harder when you are around these people. There have been people in my life who did not think that I was any smarter than I looked and were determined to make sure that I didn't get any smarter.

I've long appreciated simple honesty as one the most wonderful traits in life. Being truthful with yourself and those around you makes it possible to go through the day with a winning attitude. I think I've been successful at relating this, because no man can be more blessed with a positive family than I am. We've all learned that being honest is the right way to get ahead in life. I started in life from zero and there were times in life when I thought I was getting ahead, only to get pushed back down to zero, maybe even below. Through hard work I always came back and I can say that I excelled at the new challenges that I took on. You can never be afraid of working hard.

Don't be shy about beating your own drum when necessary. Aim for the top of the sun and, once you get there, God will always shine on you.

My beautiful daughters Patti & Lizanne